Creating Effective Groups

The Art of Small Group Communication

Randy Fujishin
WEST VALLEY COLLEGE

Acada Books
San Francisco

ALSO BY RANDY FUJISHIN
*Published by Acada Books

*Creating Communication**
*Gifts from the Heart**
The Natural Speaker

Copyeditor: David Sweet
Proofreader: Julia Bloch
Indexer: Patricia Deminna
Designer: Desktop Miracles, Inc.

Acada Books
P.O. Box 642776
San Francisco, California 94164-2776
Tel.: (415) 776-2325
info@acadabooks.com
www.acadabooks.com

Creating Effective Groups is a revised edition of *Discovering the Leader Within: Running Small Groups Successfully* (0-9655029-1-0).

Publisher's Cataloging-in Publication
(Provided by Quality Books, Inc.)

Fujishin, Randy.
    Creating effective groups : the art of small group communication / Randy Fujishin. — 1st ed.
    p. cm.
    Includes bibliographical references and index.
    ISBN: 0-9655029-9-6

    1. Communication in small groups.   2. Small groups.   3. Group decision making. I. Title.
HM133.F85 2001   302.3'4
                                                         QBI00–849

Printed on recycled paper.
Printed in the United States of America
1 2 3 4 5 — 04 03 02 01 00

Contents

Preface

WORKING IN GROUPS IS A PART of your life. *Creating Effective Groups* is designed to give a straightforward, yet comprehensive, introduction to the study of small-group communication, group decision making, group problem solving, group dynamics, leadership, or team building. You will learn the fundamental knowledge and skills necessary to communicate more effectively and interact more productively in any small group.

Creating Effective Groups includes a unique approach and pedagogical features designed to enhance learning and recall. Every chapter:

- Focuses on fundamental concepts and practical skills without getting bogged down in lengthy theoretical discussions.
- Is founded on the idea that every group member, not just the leader, contributes in significant ways to creating the task and social dimensions of any group.
- Discusses the psychological factors and variables of group interaction using the author's counseling as well as communication studies training.
- Illustrates the need for the skills and concepts presented in the chapters using real-life stories and examples.
- Employs a warm, friendly, and encouraging writing style to keep you engaged and involved in the learning process.

Creating Effective Groups provides the opportunity to practice, develop, and implement a variety of communication skills in the small-group setting so that your groups will be successful.

Whether you're the CEO of a corporation, the chairperson of a committee, a volunteer in a fund-raising group, the manager of a work team, or the head of a family reunion planning committee, you will be working with others in groups. The degree of success or failure these groups experience is, to a large extent, up to you. Your participation influences their effectiveness and productivity. Every word you utter and every gesture you make can affect other group members. One harsh word or angry glance can send a group into confusion and conflict. One kind word or gesture of support can cultivate cohesion, encourage cooperation, and even bring healing to a group. One act can change the direction and destiny of any group. You can help create an effective group regardless of the group's purpose or your assigned role.

ACKNOWLEDGMENTS

I would like to thank Brian Romer for his belief in my original manuscript and his desire to bring this book into its second edition. His vision, wisdom, and passion as a publisher will always be appreciated. My deep gratitude goes to my editor, Robin Romer, whose skillful guidance and gentle reassurance brought my manuscript to a level worthy of publication. I am deeply indebted to Brian and Robin for their talents, care, and friendship.

I would like to thank the many reviewers who read the manuscript and offered valuable comments and suggestions: Bill Baker, Brigham Young University; Robyn Bergstrom, Ricks College; Alice L. Crume, State University of New York at Brockport; Roberta A. Davilla, University of Northern Iowa; C. Jay Frasier, Lane Community College; Daniel Gerber, University of Massachusetts Amherst; Laura Johnson, Appalachian State University; Kathryn Hoge Leftwich, West Virginia University Institute of Technology; Kenneth Melichar, Piedmont College; Diane Mello-Goldner, Pine Manor College; Betsy Morgan, University of Wisconsin-La Crosse; Duane Sunwold, Spokane Community College; and Kathryn A. Wiss, Western Connecticut State University.

I would like to thank my sisters, Diane Sakayue, Melanie Cottengim, Nanette Vidales, and Teresa Gruber; my friends, Paul Sanders, Lucy Clemente, and Van and Marilyn Cummings; and my mother, Helen Fujishin, for their love and support.

Finally, I would like to thank my wife, Vicky, and our sons, Tyler and Jared. They have created the loving home that is the best place in the world for me. It is to them that I dedicate this book.

CHAPTER ONE

Working in a Group

The real voyage of discovery consists not in seeking
new landscapes, but in having new eyes.

MARCEL PROUST

THE BEST JOURNEYS IN LIFE PROVIDE US with new ways of seeing the world. Whether it's a monthlong expedition to the Himalayas or a thirty-minute visit with an old friend, we come away from the experience with a greater understanding and appreciation of others and ourselves. We are changed. With new eyes, we see that we are capable of becoming more than we once believed—that we can be freer, happier, and stronger than we once thought.

The best journeys in life, we discover, bring us closer to our truer selves.

One such journey took place for me in a cramped, cheerless conference room in Santa Barbara many years ago. I was a part-time employee at a small electronics company during my sophomore year of college, and I was asked to participate in a small group that would recommend ways to boost employee morale.

My experience with small groups was limited to high-school student government and two college group projects in psychology. All these meetings were disorganized, adversarial, and long. Invariably, one person would monopolize the discussion, while the rest of us would roll our eyes and watch the clock. We accomplished very little. At the end of these meetings, I often left the room feeling confused, frustrated, and angry.

I was not expecting to experience anything different in that small, cluttered conference room in Santa Barbara. I was the youngest of the seven-member group. The other six were full-time employees in their thirties and forties. I felt inadequate and unnecessary. Before we sat down, the team leader introduced himself to me and offered me a soft drink. Once the meeting began, I was surprised by the organized flow of the discussion. The leader skillfully kept us on track, occasionally summarized the ideas that were being considered, and often complimented us for contributing other ideas. He even asked me for my thoughts a number of times as I sat silently watching the dance of the discussion. Before I knew it, the leader was highlighting the main proposals we had generated, previewing the next step in the process, and thanking us for our work. That first meeting ended in less than one hour!

The other five meetings ran as smoothly as the first. We had moments of disagreement and conflict during the six hours, but our team leader was skillful in guiding the discussion, accepting of our differences, and insightful in focusing and synthesizing our ideas.

In the end, I no longer regarded working in groups as something to be avoided. Rather, working in groups was something that could be productive, exciting, and even fun. Because of that, I saw a different world and a different me.

This chapter will explore the basic nature and process of any small group you will participate in or lead. The most important concept to keep in mind as you work with small groups is that you, one individual member of a group, can make a difference. Your personal contributions can help make or break a group, so strive to be positive, constructive, and encouraging in all that you do. Your efforts will contribute to creating effective groups.

WORKING IN GROUPS

Human beings have gathered in groups since the beginning of recorded history because they benefit from the pooled skills, knowledge, resources, and experience provided by the group. The group, with its collective resources, usually stands a greater chance for survival and success. Of course, not every group runs as smoothly as the one I just described. In fact, working in small groups can be one of our most challenging activities. But you can learn skills and discover strengths within yourself to make this process more effective and rewarding.

Working in groups is a part of life. Whether you're the vice president of marketing, a member of a PTA group, or the head of the high-school reunion planning committee, you will be working with others in small groups.

At first glance, this activity may seem easy. All you do is sit around a table, talk, and accomplish things. What could be easier? But rather than experiencing unselfish cooperation, responsible preparation, and open communication in our group efforts, we are often shocked by the lack of cooperation, the inadequacy of preparation, and the poor communication skills of group members. If we are honest, we also have to admit to our own inabilities and lack of understanding of this complicated process.

FOUR ELEMENTS OF A SMALL GROUP

A **small group** is three or more people who share a common task, interact face-to-face, and influence one another. Let's consider each element.

Three or More People

The minimum number of individuals needed to constitute a small group is three people. Two people do not make a group because their interaction is that of a couple, or **dyad**. In a dyad, one person speaks, the other listens and responds, and then the original speaker considers what is being said. No third individual witnesses the event or influences the interaction. A dyad normally encourages more self-disclosure, simply because no audience or third party is present.

Most groups have little control over the number of participants. The size of the group may be determined by group policy, management, available people, or the size of the meeting room. Group membership can range from three to thirty people or more.

I believe the ideal number of members in a small group is five to seven. In a group this size, each member is encouraged to speak without the imposition of a large number of individuals serving as an audience. Also, a group of five to seven provides more input than smaller groups do and maintains a comfortable level of intimacy that larger groups often lack. This book examines and discusses groups of five to seven people.

Sharing a Common Task

The second essential element of a small group is that the group shares a task or problem it feels is worth solving. Whether it is brainstorming ways to generate money, selecting a candidate for a committee, or planning a coworker's retirement dinner, the group must accomplish an identified task or goal. That task is the primary purpose for the existence of the group.

Interacting Face-to-Face

The third element of a small group is that group members interact face-to-face. This means they will be able to see one another's faces. Usually this meeting will occur in the same room with all members physically present. In some cases, group members may be scattered around the country or even the world.

Video technology, videoteleconferencing, and the Internet permit group members to see and hear one another without their being physically present in the same room. Teleconferencing still satisfies our "face-to-face" criterion, although most of the nonverbal communication occurring in such interactions is lost. **Nonverbal communication** is all communication that is neither spoken nor written; it includes such variables as body movement, paralanguage, clothing, punctuality, gestures, distancing or proxemics, facial expressions, use of time, and seating arrangements. Research has consistently reminded us that nonverbal communication often has more impact on the receiver of a message than words themselves have.

> Example is not the main thing in influencing others. It is the only thing.
>
> ALBERT SCHWEITZER

Ideally, the group meets around a single table, thereby providing as much nonverbal information as possible. Being physically close to other human beings provides an immeasurable advantage as you interact and communicate. It's always better to be able to see the face and the body of the person you're interacting with, rather than hearing a tinny voice over a phone receiver, because without the nonverbal cues, much information about content and speaker can be lost.

Influencing One Another

This final element is fundamental to a small group. A group member does not exist and operate in a vacuum, isolated from the other members. Each member's statements and behavior affect every other group member in some way, be it small or great. A thoughtful compliment, a subtle criticism, a raised eyebrow, or a complaining moan can communicate a message of monumental proportions, and its effect can last a lifetime.

You can learn from other members' information and grow from their suggestions; be persuaded by their arguments and challenged by their proposals; be hurt by their remarks and healed by their praises. You can be deflated by other members' bickering and inspired by their encouragement. Each member influences and is influenced by other group members, whether he or she realizes this fact.

THE SMALL GROUP AS A SYSTEM

A common illusion is that we are separate from the other members of the group. We often tend to see our individual needs, behaviors, responses, and communication as disconnected from those of our group members. Most of our behavior and thinking are self-motivated, and we often lack awareness of the intricate and profound connections the group has established in its web of interactions.

There are two ways to look at group interactions. The first way sees group members as distinct and disconnected from any substantial and meaningful tie with the other people, like lone cow-

> We are all connected
> to one another in ways
> both large and small. To deny
> this is to turn your back on
> one of life's greatest truths.
> KARL MENNINGER

boys meeting on a hill to chat and then galloping off in different directions. In other words, I enter into the group being me, and I leave the group being me. Nothing has changed in me, except that I've spent some time with other people.

The second way views group interaction as if the group were a living organism. Each member is a part of this living organism. You're the heart, I'm the lungs, and the other members serve their respective functions of the body. When something happens to one part, all the other parts feel the effects. This is the essence of the systems perspective of group interaction.

A **system** is a collection of interdependent parts arrayed in such a way that a change in one component will affect changes in all the other components. The emphasis in a systems perspective is not on the individual, but rather on the group as a whole. Any group of people working together to solve a problem meets this definition of a system. Four characteristics of a system—interdependence, mutual influence, adaptation, and equifinality—are valuable in understanding and appreciating the small-group process.

Interdependence

Interdependence means that each group member depends on all the other members in some way. An obvious example is the absence of four of the five members from a meeting. Even though you are present, the absence of the other group members makes it impossible for you to participate in the meeting. Another example is a group member who doesn't research or produce a critical piece of information the group needs to proceed. One member's behavior, or lack of behavior, prevents the entire group from progressing. In many ways, you are connected to and dependent on the actions of the other group members.

Yet once the individual members form a working group, they acquire a collective life. The group can take on characteristics—productivity, creativity, and responsiveness—that may not be characteristic of any one member. The individuals can often become energized by the collective whole. They can achieve more productivity than any member could realize alone. This is often referred to as **synergy**—the group product is usually superior to the best individual product. In other words, two heads are better than one.

Mutual Influence

Mutual influence implies that cause and effect are interchangeable. Each action or behavior serves as both a response to a previous behavior and a stimulus for a future action. This characteristic of systems theory makes it pointless to attempt to assign blame for any problematic behavior because that behavior was in response to a previous behavior. An example of this is the "nag/withdraw" syndrome. A wife withdraws because her husband nags. But the husband insists he nags because she withdraws. Oftentimes it is pointless to assign blame, to point the finger at who started the whole mess, because the behaviors are so intertwined. Rather than blame, the wife and the husband should explore ways to alter or modify the pattern of "nag/withdraw." The focus is on modifying behavior patterns instead of seeking to blame or punish.

Adaptation

Adaptation means that a system will seek to adapt to fit the demands of a changing environment. The group's flexibility to modify its procedures, rules, communication patterns, and even its way of thinking and feeling is indicative of its ability to survive and is required for its overall health. The group must remain flexible and willing to transform in order to cope with the changing environment (people, issues, and circumstances). Groups that are rigid, dogmatic, and unwilling to explore and discover new ways of operating are doomed to mediocrity and often failure. The flexible group is a healthy group.

Equifinality

Equifinality is the ability of a group to accomplish a goal in many ways and from many starting points. The group must accept the fact that there are many ways to accomplish a goal or task, not just one right way. The concept of equifinality opens up the possibility and potential for creative approaches to solving problems, which includes seeing the "problem" from a variety of viewpoints. Many roads lead to the "good life." The secret is discovering the one that feels right to you.

THE POWER OF ONE

Every behavior of each individual has its effect on the group—regardless of whether the behavior is negative and counterproductive, or positive and productive. In other words, your behavior, whether negative or positive, influences the group's interaction and final product. The beauty of a systems perspective on group process is that it serves to remind you that you have the power to influence and determine the direction and outcome of the group.

Peter Senge supports this idea of the Power of One in his book *The Fifth Discipline: The Art and Practice of the Learning Organization*. Senge believes that systems thinking is the key to understanding how groups and organizations work—the idea that all the parts of a group or organization are ultimately connected to one another and that "low leverage change can shift large structures within an organization." Senge encourages us to discover ways to participate and contribute in small ways to actually affect and change large organizations and institutions. Your participation can play a very important role in creating an effective group.

CHARACTERISTICS OF GROUPS

To better understand how your individual participation influences the effectiveness of a group, you need to become familiar with the basic characteristics of groups.

Group Formation

Whenever I see a group of businesspeople in a meeting, a cluster of Boy Scouts pitching tents at a campground, or a group of protesters picketing city hall, I am reminded why individuals join others to form groups—because all members receive something personally from their affiliation with the group. People join groups for a variety of reasons.

Author Will Schutz feels that three basic needs motivate individuals to become members of a group: inclusion, control, and affection.

Inclusion is people's need to feel wanted or to be a part of something bigger than themselves. They want to feel "in" and not "left out." The need for inclusion describes the desire to belong, to fit in, to be valued, and to be. We want to count, to matter. Inclusion in a group can often validate our worth in the world.

People want to be included in certain groups because they are attracted to the group's activities or even to the group members—not attraction in the sense of romance and love, but in terms of likeness and affinity. They often join groups because of similarity in beliefs, ethnicity, economic status, or age. People join religious, social activist, or flying-saucer clubs because of common beliefs. Others join groups such as the Japanese American Citizenship League, the NAACP, and the Mexican American Youth Association for their ethnic similarities. Membership in a country club, the Millionaires Club, or a homeless shelter can be motivated by economic likeness. An individual may join a group to participate in its activities. Groups such as a social dancing club, a fraternity or sorority, a weight-lifting group, and a bird-watching club provide opportunities for people to gather with others and feel included.

Many people join groups to discover or strengthen their identity and purpose for living. We determine our self-identity to a great extent by the people with whom we associate. Birds of a feather often flock together. Many of the groups identified above—religious or social organizations, businesses, and even the Hell's Angels—can provide a person with a strong sense of identity and purpose.

Control provides individuals with the sense that they have some degree of personal influence and power over their environment, that what they say and do makes a difference in the decisions and activities of the group as well as in other facets of life. Participation in a small group can provide individuals with opportunities to share opinions and feelings, to influence and persuade others, and to solve problems.

Many people join groups so that they can experience some degree of influence and contribution. The goal or objective the group seeks to achieve can provide this sense of influence and contribution. Groups such as a volunteer wilderness rescue team, a Little League fund-raising group, a corporate work team, or a politician's election campaign provide opportunities for individuals to help advance a cause or accomplish a goal. Once the goal is achieved, the group often disbands. But this isn't necessarily so. Examples of long-term groups are Mothers Against Drunk Drivers (MADD), Alcoholics Anonymous (AA), and Greenpeace: these groups give individuals the sense that they can make a difference for a lifetime.

Affection, the need to be liked and the ability to initiate and maintain close relationships with others, might be the most basic of Schutz's three interpersonal needs that motivate people to join groups. Humans have the need to form close friendships and ties with others. Without giving and receiving love and affection, our lives would be dull indeed. Oftentimes, participation in groups can provide people with some level of affection. The interpersonal relationships you form during group work can be enjoyable, rewarding, and growing experiences in and of themselves. A friendship you make in a group may turn into a lifelong relationship. Who knows what can develop when you join a group?

You might have noticed some groups satisfy more than one of the three basic needs for joining groups. For example, a religious organization can provide inclusion, control, and affection. This is true for the majority of groups that people join—there is rarely only one reason for group affiliation.

Although many of these groups are not necessarily problem-solving groups, they provide ample opportunities to make decisions and solve problems. Even a social dancing club will occasionally plan a fundraiser, arrange a dance with other clubs, or decide what to do with a member who makes others uncomfortable with overt flirting.

Task and Social Dimensions of Groups

Once membership in a group is established, interaction within the group occurs in two areas or dimensions—the task dimension and the social dimension. Each dimension covers a different aspect and purpose of the group's interactions.

Task dimension. Each group must attempt to complete some action or solve a problem. All the group's work or efforts to this end are considered the **task dimension** of a group. Researching the problem, analyzing the problem, brainstorming solutions, discussing the strengths and weaknesses of the solutions, reaching consensus on the best solution, and implementing the solution are all elements of the group's task dimension.

Social dimension. While the group is busy doing its work in the task dimension, the social dimension is occurring simultaneously. The

social dimension is the interpersonal relationships of the group members; it consists of their feelings and interactions. The social dimension is not separate from the task dimension, but rather is intertwined in it. A change in one produces a change in the other. We don't really understand all the subtle relationships between the task dimension and the social dimension, but we can be certain they do influence each other.

Norms and Conformity

In every group, the behavior of all group members is determined and regulated to a great extent by the norms operating at the explicit and implicit levels. Conformity or adherence to these norms provides many benefits to the group. Challenging group norms can be an important task of the effective group member.

Norms. The rules that regulate the behavior of group members, **norms** provide the basic building blocks of group interaction. They hold the group together, making smooth, predictable interaction possible. Without norms of behavior, the group could easily be thrust into confusion, alienation, and even hostility. **Implicit norms** are norms understood by group members, either consciously or unconsciously, but not announced verbally or in writing by the group. Norms such as keeping quiet when others are speaking, being polite, sitting face-to-face with other members, and avoiding obscenities are examples of implicit rules or norms. **Explicit norms** are norms orally stated or written down as a code of conduct or expected group behavior. Many groups will establish formal rules of behavior that members are expected to follow. For example, military organizations, weight-reduction groups, and religious sects might provide new group members with a list of expected behaviors, either verbally or in writing.

Conformity to norms. Conformity is the adherence to group norms. Why do group members obey or adhere to the norms of the group? There are many reasons. First, conformity to norms makes life easier, orderly, predictable, and organized. For example, rather than always having to consider and decide from circumstance to circumstance when to talk, whom to face, and which hand to shake, group members can follow norms that prescribe these behaviors. Second, adherence to norms makes the interactions within the group more productive. Rather than spending time debating which behaviors are acceptable and which are unacceptable, the group can direct its efforts to the task dimension. Third, conformity to norms provides each member with a sense of belonging and acceptance. Whether the group has a secret group handshake, a moose lodge hat, or a certain style of dress, norms of behavior can make you feel like one of the group.

Clarifying a norm. When you are in doubt about an ambiguous or confusing implicit norm, ask the group for clarification. For instance, assume that most group members, including the leader, arrived late for the past three meetings, but you were punctual. Bring the implicit norm (arriving late to meetings is acceptable) to the group for discussion. You could say, "I've noticed many group members

> It is by risking
> that we live at all.
> W I L L I A M   J A M E S

arrive ten to fifteen minutes after our agreed-upon meeting time. Is this the accepted norm of the group? I need clarification on this, because if it is the accepted norm, I too will arrive late."

Most group members are not used to having implicit norms brought to the explicit level of oral discussion. Many issues of substantive and interpersonal conflict can be resolved during the early stages of group development if the group puts the issue on the table for all to see and discuss. Don't be afraid to make the invisible visible.

Challenging a norm. It's also important for you and the group to challenge any explicit norm you feel is illegal, unethical, or harmful to group members or others. History is filled with examples of men and women who without question or challenge followed the rules or norms of a group that brought pain and suffering to others. Just as you can clarify an implicit norm, you can challenge an explicit norm before the group. This requires some courage, because you may be challenging the leadership and power structure of the group. But if you feel deep in your heart that a particular norm is harming others, you owe it to yourself and others to speak.

STAGES OF GROUP DEVELOPMENT

Every group changes during the course of its existence. It has a life all its own. No two groups are exactly the same. The following are two perspectives of group development.

Perspective 1: Four Phases of Group Development

Aubrey Fisher identified a four-phase sequence of group development that consists of periods of orientation, conflict, emergence, and reinforcement.

Orientation. Most members of new groups spend their first meeting or two getting to know one another. Group members often feel a high level of anxiety and uncertainty because they have little or no previous history together. The orientation phase is devoted to letting the group members "break the ice" and get acquainted. Humorous remarks, polite behavior, social chitchat, and conflict avoidance are characteristic of this group-development phase. This phase is often referred to as **primary tension**—the uneasiness group members feel because they are unfamiliar with one another. The social dimension of the group is overemphasized during this time because the establishment of a warm, supportive, and trusting environment is crucial to the group's task dimension in later phases of its development.

It is also during the orientation phase that members initiate discussion about the nature and scope of the task before them. Group members will often state their opinions and feelings in tentative, vague language, because they may not yet be comfortable fully disclosing their positions on issues.

The group is not just "spinning its wheels" or wasting time during the orientation phase. It is actually establishing a foundation of group member knowledge and interaction that will make the group perform more effectively in the later phases.

Conflict. After group members are comfortable enough to share their opinions and feelings at a deeper level, they begin the second phase of group process: the conflict phase. Conflict is a natural and expected part of group process because it is during this phase that group members begin to express their individual opinions and feelings. They discuss the nature and background of the problem, propose solutions, debate the relative merits of the solutions, and select the best solution or solutions. During the conflict phase, group members begin to clarify their opinions and feelings about the issues. They devote more energy to sharing differences of opinion, arguing positions, and debating the issues. It is also during this phase that members critically evaluate evidence presented and the reasoning for the solutions proposed. Uneasiness experienced here is called **secondary tension**—the tension caused by disagreement or criticism over one's ideas, evidence, or proposed solutions.

Groups that develop a safe, supportive social dimension during the orientation phase are more likely to successfully weather the secondary tension experienced during the conflict phase. Groups that have not devoted sufficient time to the orientation phase can buckle under the pressures of conflict. Conversely, groups that have developed an overly cohesive social dimension may see conflict as a threat to their tight-knit, happy family and will avoid the conflict that is necessary to be effective in the task dimension. The concept of groupthink is discussed in greater detail in Chapter 9.

Emergence. During the third phase, group members move from debate and conflict to a possible solution that is acceptable to all members. It's a time when the group negotiates, compromises, and begins to discover common ground. Whereas the conflict phase emphasizes differences of opinion, the emergence phase focuses on similarities. During this phase, decisions emerge. Members increasingly make statements of agreement, acceptance, and approval and then decide on or adopt a solution.

Reinforcement. The final phase occurs when group members congratulate themselves on a job well done. During this time, the group also constructs an implementation plan and timetable for the agreed-upon solution. The social dimension is reinforced in this phase with the expression of positive feelings about the group and its accomplishments. Members often feel a strong sense of group identity and belonging. Disagreement, conflicts, and arguments were successfully negotiated and the group is stronger and more effective because of it.

If you've ever worked in small groups, however, you know that they rarely follow the exact steps Fisher identified. A group may go through these phases for each issue it addresses. One group might devote the majority of its time to orientation and socializing, whereas another group will bypass orientation altogether and focus solely on the task at hand. Groups can get sidetracked, abandon their discussion, or disband altogether. In real life, the journey a small group takes is much more complex and the stages it experiences are not as clear-cut.

Perspective 2: Multiple Sequence Model of Group Development

To more accurately account for this complexity, Marshall Poole described group development not as a linear model, but as a multiple sequence model of decision emergence. This model of group process envisions a group moving along three activity tracks—task, relational, and topic. The **task track** is the structure or the phase of the discussion, the **relational track** is the social dimension of the group, and the **topic track** is the specific issue or content of the discussion at that moment.

A group on the task track may decide to return to the analysis of the problem, take a vote on an issue, or postpone discussion of an item. A group on the relational track focuses and interacts on the social dimension of the group, sharing personal information, taking a break, or joking with one another. Finally, the topic track is the actual discussion of the task issue the group is attempting to solve, such as sharing information and evidence, questioning, negotiating, and reaching consensus.

Groups do not necessarily move along the three tracks in this model at the same rate or in the same way. Some groups invest a great amount of time in the relational track before moving to the task track, while other groups may focus primarily on the task track and devote minimal time to the relational track. Breakpoints are the transitions when groups switch activity tracks.

Fisher's four phases of group development and Poole's multiple sequence model provide helpful insights into the life and activity of small groups. Fisher helps us understand and establish goals for group work. Poole indicates that groups don't always proceed along a single, predictable path, but rather shift the focus of group activity depending on the group's needs. Specific goals of group development and flexibility in the attainment of those goals are important to remember as you work with others.

This chapter provided you with a basic understanding of small-group process, and, more importantly, explained how groups operate systemically. When you participate in any group, keep in mind the reasons why people join groups, the dimensions of group interaction, and the stages of group development. Working in a group is no easy matter; these basic concepts will enable you to participate in groups in constructive, positive, and caring ways so you can help create a more effective group.

INDIVIDUAL AND GROUP EXERCISES

1.1 Family of Origin Rules

Consider what your life was like growing up in your family of origin—your original group. Did your parents plaster rules to the refrigerator and the bathroom mirrors? Did you receive long lectures about what to do and what not to do? Or did your parents even talk to you? Make a list of five spoken (explicit) or unspoken (implicit) rules or norms of behavior you remember from your family of origin. Be as specific as possible.

Could you list five rules from your family of origin? What did you think of them? What did you think of them when you were a kid? Do you still operate under these communication rules as an adult? Examine the rules you listed. Do you see any that could interfere with how you communicate today?

1.2 Small Group Permission List

The following statements pertain to some aspect of communication or interaction in a small group. Read each statement, and then indicate whether you agree or disagree with it, using the ratings below. Respond to each statement based on what you think about your communication behavior, not on what others have said.

(1=strongly disagree, 2=disagree, 3=unsure, 4=agree, 5=strongly agree)

I give myself permission to:

1.	Participate in a small group.	1 2 3 4 5
2.	Share my thoughts and ideas with the group.	1 2 3 4 5
3.	Share my feelings with the group.	1 2 3 4 5
4.	Disagree with other group members.	1 2 3 4 5
5.	Listen to the opposing ideas of other members.	1 2 3 4 5
6.	Listen to criticism from other members.	1 2 3 4 5
7.	Respond to criticism from other members.	1 2 3 4 5
8.	Consider points of view different from my own.	1 2 3 4 5
9.	Compromise when it will benefit the group.	1 2 3 4 5
10.	Facilitate negotiation within the group.	1 2 3 4 5

How did you rate yourself on these statements? You need to discover how you feel about each behavior if you work in a group for any length of time. Think about each item before you enter into any group process.

1.3 Sharing in Your Group

In your small group, share your findings from Exercise 1.2. Prepare a one- or two-minute statement that summarizes your response to this exercise; highlight three strengths and three weaknesses you see in yourself. When others share their responses and lists, refrain from judging or evaluating them. Simply listen and learn.

CHAPTER TWO

Discovering Yourself

Knowing the self is enlightenment.

LAO TSU

THE MORNING SUN FEELS WARM on my face. There is no sound, no movement, only a gravel road stretching in a straight line for twenty miles in either direction, like a gray ribbon disappearing into the distance. I'm sitting on the tailgate of my pickup, listening to the silence of the desert, somewhere between Tonopah, Nevada, and the Utah border.

This is my second day in the desert. Last night I camped about three miles from here, on a smooth ridge overlooking this valley. Most of the evening I sat in my beach chair and gazed at the stars overhead. I made no fire. I played no music. I simply sat and watched the stars, as the gentle breeze came up from the southwest. I listened to the silence all around.

I find the desert silence beautiful. Like a celestial choir from a distant galaxy, its anthem speaks to my heart, calms my body, and once again I hear my own breathing deep and true. I soon discover my thinking ceases and my heart expands to greet the silent stars above.

The solitude of the desert puts me in touch with myself. Far from the responsibilities of family and friends, work and community, I can sit and breathe. And do nothing for a time.

Once or twice a year I venture into the desert alone for two or three nights. Leaving the comfort of my wife and children, and all that is familiar, I withdraw from my regular life. The experience replenishes my spirit. It makes me feel whole, alive, and connected to those things that give my life meaning upon my return.

The desert experience also enables me to detach a little more from my usual tendency to want to control others—especially the students I teach, the families I counsel, and the trainees I instruct at industry seminars. I've discovered that I return from the desert with a stronger desire to watch the process of the group unfold, rather than force my own agenda. I am more willing to listen to the opinions and feelings of others, rather than advocate or advance my own position. I have gotten in touch with a quieter, deeper part of who I am, the part of me that isn't rattled or shaken by debate, disagreement, criticism, or conflict. This enhances my ability to face the rigors and requirements of small-group work.

Working with others in a small group can be one of the most demanding, challenging, and often frustrating tasks you perform. The proximity, the different personalities, the heated discussions, the misunderstandings, large and small, can and do provide the ingredients for all kinds of conflict within any group. If you do not possess some degree of perspective, self-awareness, and calm, the rigors of working with others can quickly get the best of you. This chapter will provide you with the opportunity to know yourself a little better.

BEING OPEN TO SELF-DISCOVERY

Before you can be open to the ideas, opinions, and feelings of others, you must first be open to your own ideas, opinions, and feelings. This might seem obvious at first glance. Of course you're open to your own thoughts and feelings. Who knows you better than you? But do you really?

It has been my experience while training, leading, and working with groups that most people go into a small group with a limited level of self-awareness and self-knowledge. During the course of group work, little things irritate them without their realizing that they do the same things. They are upset by the different opinions of others. They are hurt when someone criticizes them. They are frustrated when someone interrupts them in midsentence. They get angry when the group doesn't decide in their favor. Sound familiar? It is as if the entire world has to agree for us to be happy. If not, we're upset.

Very rarely will the other group members see the world the way you do. In fact, the more you listen to the ideas and opinions of others, the more you'll realize just how different we all are.

So, are you destined to be frustrated, angry, and hopeless while you work in groups? Not at all. But working in groups requires that you open yourself to a little self-discovery before you enter into the wild world of working with other humans. To know yourself—your strengths as well as your weaknesses, your beauty as well as your ugliness—is helpful in getting to know others.

When was the last time you discovered something new about yourself? Maybe you recently broke off a friendship because you realized you didn't want to invest the energy the relationship required. Perhaps you enrolled in an art class and discovered you enjoy painting with watercolors. Or maybe you watched a documentary on television and found yourself for the first time in your life thoroughly engrossed in the history of the Japanese samurai warriors. Every day you have countless opportunities to discover fascinating, beautiful, and even surprising things about yourself—if you are open.

However, many people are closed to new discoveries about themselves and the world around them. There's a story about a college professor of religion who visited a Zen priest. The old priest invited the young professor to sit down in his simple yet tasteful room. The professor immediately began talking about Zen. He talked and talked. The old priest began to pour tea into the professor's cup as the young man droned on. Even after the cup was full, the priest continued to pour the tea. The cup overflowed, and the tea eventually spilled on the young man's lap.

The professor shouted, "Master, why are you still pouring the tea? Can't you see the cup is already full?"

"You are very observant," replied the priest. "The same is true for you. If you are to receive any of my teachings, you must first empty the cup of your mind, for it is already full of your old learnings."

Like the professor, we are not always open to self-discovery, or any kind of discovery for that matter, because we are full of old learnings. Old learning can be any idea we have about ourselves and who we think we are. The majority of these ideas came from others—parents, teachers, coaches, friends, and acquaintances—as well as from movies, television, radio, magazines, and books, telling us who we should be and what we should want.

Very little of our learning comes from deep within ourselves, because we spend few of our waking moments completely alone with our thoughts and feelings. Television and music blare around us. Phones surround us. We avoid spending an evening alone. But we can benefit from taking time to discover who we believe we are, rather than who everyone else says we are. Without this fundamental knowledge, your interactions with others will lack connection, depth, and maturity. Spending time by yourself is the most powerful way to accomplish this goal.

SPENDING TIME BY YOURSELF

Not everyone has the desire or the time to go off to the desert for several days of solitude. But I believe there are countless other ways we can experience periods of solitude in our daily lives. Spending time by yourself doesn't necessarily require a solo trip to the Himalayas or joining a Benedictine monastery. Solitude can be discovered right where you are, if you are open to it. The following suggestions provide five simple ways you can experience solitude. Don't feel that you have to try them. But if you'd like to get a feel for who you are without the interruption of others, you might want to try one or two of these activities. I think you'll enjoy them.

> All of the troubles of life
> come upon us because
> we refuse to sit quietly for a
> while each day in our rooms.
> BLAISE PASCAL

Waking Up Earlier

No matter how busy or cramped your life is, give yourself the gift of ten minutes of solitude by waking up earlier in the morning. Experiment with your morning ritual by setting the alarm ten minutes earlier for one week. Instead of waking up at 6:30, try 6:20. That may not sound too appealing, but you'll discover you're much more flexible than you thought. Use those extra ten minutes to sit in the kitchen or living room and watch the sunrise, listen to the birds sing, or hum a song of your own, while the rest of the world sleeps.

Going to Bed Later

Try going to bed ten minutes later in the evening, especially if you're a night owl. So, instead of going to bed at 11:00, you hit the sack at 11:10. During those extra ten minutes, do nothing. Bundle up in a big coat, sit in the backyard or on the roof (don't fall off!), and look at the stars overhead. Don't do anything. Just sit. This is your gift to yourself.

Taking Time Out

During the course of your day, give yourself a ten-minute minivacation by taking time out to stroll around outside the office or on campus, instead of visiting with your colleagues at the water cooler or the snack shop. This ritual can become the most peaceful and restful ten minutes of your workday.

Turning Off the Radio and the Phone

Another way you can be alone is to turn off the radio or stereo (and the cellular phone) when driving to and from work. It's amazing how different your driving experience can be without the constant intrusion of other people's voices and music. In the silence you will hear other things. I think you'll be surprised by the experience.

Stopping for Decompression Time

Returning home from a day at work or school also provides an opportunity to give yourself the gift of solitude. I call it decompression time. Usually, we rush out of work or school, fight the traffic for thirty to sixty minutes, skid into our driveway, and rush into the house, only to be met by family or roommates. We do all this without a quiet transition or decompression time. Try doing it differently for a while. Before pulling up to your driveway after a day at work or school, stop at a nearby park, an elementary school, or a quiet spot in the neighborhood for ten minutes to catch your breath, collect yourself, and decompress before entering the next phase of your daily life. This can transform you back into a pleasant, even charming individual whose arrival at the end of the day will be anticipated with joy!

These are just five simple things you can do to give yourself the gift of solitude. You can probably brainstorm a number of other creative ways to incorporate a little alone time. Don't forget the traditional ways of experiencing solitude, such as a solo afternoon trip to the lake, an overnight safari, meditation, prayer, or a stroll through the neighborhood after dinner. No matter what form of solitude you select, the important point is to get away from the hustle and bustle of life and open yourself to your own music.

I've discovered in my work with small groups that individuals who experience the greatest amount of disagreement, conflict, and hostility with others are often those people who are in conflict with themselves. Their relationships with others tell me a great deal about their relationships with themselves.

We need to be at peace with ourselves before we can be at peace with others. One of the best ways to begin this journey is to spend time alone before entering any group process. Once you have experienced solitude, you can begin to discover some things about yourself.

SELF-DISCOVERY INVENTORIES

There are countless ways to discover things about yourself. Personality tests, IQ scores, feedback from family and friends, report cards, job reviews, handwriting analysis, and career placement tests are but a few of the hundreds of methods people use to provide you with information about who they think you are. Advertisements in magazines, billboards, television, and radio, as well as the heroes in the evening news, movies, and paperbacks, also provide a steady diet of images of who we should strive to emulate if we are to be worthwhile, desirable, and loved. The information from "out there" telling us who we are and who we should be is never-ending.

> The unexamined life
> is not worth living.
> S O C R A T E S

Leave these sources of information that claim to know who you are and who you should be for a moment and look to yourself for the same information. You will not know all there is to know about yourself after completing these inventories, but you will become more familiar with yourself.

Inventory 1: Who Are You?

Complete the following statements with the first idea, noun, adjective, verb, and so on that comes to mind. Don't think about your response; just jot it down. Give yourself only sixty seconds.

1. I am _Sensitive_.
2. I am _fun-loving_.
3. I am _adventurous_.
4. I am _intuitive_.
5. I am _Thoughtful_.

Were you able to write down five responses about who you are? Do you notice any patterns in your responses? For instance, are most of your responses nouns (roles) such as student, wife, Buddhist, engineer, secretary, cowboy, or brain surgeon? Or are most of your responses descriptions such as caring, loving, resentful, lonely, twenty-seven years old, redheaded, or inquisitive? Are there any characteristics or roles you listed that are essential to who you are? Are there any you would like to change or modify? How do you see your responses affecting your interaction with other individuals and groups?

Inventory 2: What Do You Believe?

Complete the following statements with a belief you hold. Take a bit more time to consider each response than you did in Inventory 1. Give yourself five minutes.

1. I believe _in laughing as much as possible_.
2. I believe _in doing something I love_.
3. I believe _in not giving-up_.
4. I believe _in speaking my truth_.
5. I believe _in travelling as much as possible_

Were you able to write down five beliefs? If not, what does this mean to you? Do you notice any patterns in your responses? Do your beliefs concern yourself, other people, ideas, or things? Are your beliefs stated positively or negatively? If someone held the opposite opinion or belief, how would you feel about the person? If someone held the same opinion or belief, how would you feel about the person? How do you see your beliefs affecting your interaction with other individuals and groups?

Inventory 3: Six Months to Live

Write down five things you would like to do if you discovered you had only six months to live. Assume you will experience no physical pain until the final week of life.

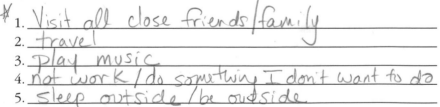

1. _Visit all close friends/family_
2. _travel_
3. _play music_
4. _not work / do something I don't want to do_
5. _sleep outside / be outside_

Do any of your responses surprise you? How do you feel about your responses? Do your responses involve people, places, or things? Which item would you most want to accomplish before dying? If you were going to die in six months, how would that affect your communication with others? How would it affect your attitude toward working with a group?

Inventory 4: Your Communication Behaviors

Read the following statements carefully; then circle the number that most accurately describes your response to the statement. Base your response on what you think, not on what others have said about your communication behavior.

(1=strongly disagree, 2=disagree, 3=unsure, 4=agree, 5=strongly agree)

1.	I speak in a pleasant tone of voice.	1 2 3 ④ 5
2.	I speak at an adequate rate (speed) of speech.	1 2 3 ④ 5
3.	I speak without verbal fillers ("um," "like," etc.).	1 2 ③ 4 5
4.	I have a relaxed posture when speaking.	1 2 ③ 4 5
5.	I use expressive gestures when speaking.	1 2 3 4 ⑤
6.	I smile when I speak with others.	1 2 3 4 ⑤
7.	I make eye contact when speaking with others.	1 2 3 4 ⑤
8.	I often nod my head in agreement when listening.	1 2 3 4 ⑤
9.	I share my opinions with close friends.	1 2 3 4 ⑤
10.	I share my opinions with acquaintances/associates.	1 2 3 ④ 5
11.	I share my feelings with close friends.	1 2 3 4 ⑤
12.	I share my feelings with acquaintances/associates.	1 2 3 ④ 5
13.	I share my needs with close friends.	1 2 3 4 ⑤
14.	I share my needs with acquaintances/associates.	1 2 3 ④ 5
15.	I am comfortable when I disagree with others.	1 2 3 ④ 5
16.	I can disagree without disliking others.	1 2 3 ④ 5
17.	I can verbally admit I'm wrong.	1 2 3 ④ 5
18.	I can ask for forgiveness when I have hurt others.	1 2 3 ④ 5
19.	I make others feel good about themselves.	1 2 3 ④ 5
20.	I am optimistic and positive in my interactions.	1 2 3 ④ 5

Statements 1 through 3 examine your voice. Statements 4 through 8 look at your nonverbal communication when interacting with others. Statements 9 through 14 examine your ability and willingness to disclose your thoughts and feelings to different people. Statements 15 through 18 focus on your behavior and attitudes when you are in disagreement or conflict with others; they also examine your ability to admit mistakes. Statements 19 and 20 look at your overall attitude and impact on others. Do you see any categories of communication behavior in which you are especially strong? Are there any categories in which you are weak or could use improvement? How would your weaknesses affect communication with others in group work? How do you feel about your overall communication skill level?

Inventory 5: You Are Not Perfect

List five communication behaviors, personal habits, personality characteristics, relationships, and anything else you can think of that you feel
need improvement. Solicit input from family and friends, coworkers
and neighbors. Just the mere fact you would ask others for feedback
will change your relationship with them.

1. I don't listen fully (jump on peoples sentences)
2. impatient (with self especially)
3. high / unreasonable expectations of self & others
4. procrastinator
5. too critical

How did you do on this inventory? I hope that you were able to identify five specific weaknesses or shortcomings. Once you can admit
you're not perfect and there are things you need to improve, the criticism or threat of criticism from others will have less impact on you.
Once you can freely admit to one weakness (or all five!), and not
invest great amounts of energy and time defending or denying your
weakness, you may experience a new freedom that allows you to be
more open to the communication and feedback of others.

Inventory 6: Your Thanksgiving List

List two things you are thankful for about your physical self, two things
you are thankful for about your psychological self, and two things you
are thankful for about your spiritual self. Choose conditions or attributes
you already possess, not those you are striving or hoping to achieve.

1. I'm thankful for my (physical) _strength_ .
2. I'm thankful for my (physical) _health_ .
3. I'm thankful for my (psychological) _sense of humor_ .
4. I'm thankful for my (psychological) _courage_ .
5. I'm thankful for my (spiritual) _Spiritual practice_ .
6. I'm thankful for my (spiritual) _intuition / guidance_ .

Was it easy or difficult to think of six things to be thankful for? If you
found it difficult, you may not have taken enough time to be aware of
and appreciate all the things that are working in your life. There are
countless things about our bodies, minds, and hearts worth appreciating and being thankful for, but we are usually too busy to take time
out to marvel at all the wonderful gifts we already possess.

SPEAKING KINDLY TO YOURSELF

In your journey to increased self-awareness, you always run the risk of discovering thoughts, ideas, and feelings that are not positive, enlarging, or encouraging. These negative thoughts can often bring us down, interfere with our communication with others, and, in general, make our lives miserable. Oftentimes, these negative thoughts not only disrupt our participation and effectiveness in group work, but also hinder our level of self-acceptance and personal growth.

In his book *A Guide to Rational Living*, psychologist Albert Ellis outlines the ten most troubling thoughts Americans have that make their lives unsatisfactory, frustrating, and depressing. He calls them our ten irrational beliefs, and I believe that many of these commonly held ideas prevent us from communicating and interacting in effective and healthy ways with others in our group work. See if you hold any of these irrational beliefs:

1. You should be liked/loved by everyone.
2. You should be competent, adequate, and achieving in all possible respects if you are to consider yourself worthwhile.
3. Happiness is externally caused and people have little or no ability to control their sorrows and disturbances.
4. Your past history is an all-important determinant of your present behavior and because something once strongly affected your life, it should indefinitely have a similar effect.
5. There is only one right solution to a problem and it is catastrophic if this perfect solution is not found.
6. If something is or may be dangerous or fearsome, you should be terribly concerned about it and should keep dwelling on the possibility of its occurring.
7. Certain people are wicked and they should always be severely blamed and punished for their villainy.
8. It is awful and catastrophic when things are not the way you would like them to be.
9. It is easier to avoid than to face certain life difficulties and self-responsibilities.
10. One should become quite upset over other people's problems and disturbances.

Ellis discovered that almost all of the psychological and emotional distress his clients were experiencing were based upon one or more of these ten irrational beliefs. In fact, irrational beliefs 1 and 2—one should be liked by everyone and one should be competent in all possible respects—accounted for almost 70 percent of his clients' presenting problems in therapy.

Ellis instructs us to identify any irrational belief we might hold, challenge that belief with its opposite idea, and ultimately replace the old belief with a healthier belief. Maybe you have told yourself one or two of the statements listed above. Or maybe you believe one of these ideas to be true for you. If so, you may want to challenge that particular belief and substitute a different, more rational belief for the irrational one you might be holding.

Here are the ten statements presented in their opposite form. Read over the list and see if any of the ideas are helpful in creating a new way of talking kindly to yourself and increasing your level of acceptance, understanding, and effectiveness when communicating with others in your group work.

1. *You don't have to be approved of by everyone. Not everyone has to like or love you.* It is irrational to strive for universal approval or affection. No one is liked, loved, or approved of by everyone. To strive to be approved of by everyone in your group is not a desirable goal. People who try to win the approval of everyone will often sacrifice their own principles, values, and happiness to placate or satisfy others.

2. *You do not have to be perfect or competent in everything you do.* No human being is perfect. There will be some activities in which you will achieve competency, even mastery, but no one is competent in everything. In fact, experiencing failure can be one of the best teachers you will ever have as you work with others in small groups.

3. *Your happiness comes from within and you can change your feelings by changing your thinking.* Your feelings are determined by your thinking, not by external events. You can change your feelings by changing your thinking. In fact, almost all the negative feelings you experience can be modified or eliminated by seeing the truth of these ten beliefs.

4. *Your current behavior is not determined by the past.* Human beings can unlearn old behaviors and replace them with new behaviors. Although many habitual ways of behaving and thinking can be deeply rooted and difficult to change, they can be

changed with focused thinking and concentrated effort. So, if your past small-group experiences have been frustrating or unsuccessful, you can open to the fact that your future group experiences can be very successful and rewarding. The past is the past. You create the present and the future!

5. *Many solutions exist for any given problem.* It's irrational to think there is only one solution to any problem. Most likely, any problem can be solved in a variety of ways. Remember the notion of equifinality from Chapter 1? There exist many ways to solve any problem. This is one belief that requires your creativity when working in a group.

6. *Don't worry.* It's irrational to worry and be overly concerned about every little thing that can go wrong in your life. The vast majority of the things you will worry about during your lifetime will never come to pass. Much of your worry is born from fatigue and loneliness. Get enough sleep, rest, and relaxation. Participate positively and optimistically when you interact with others.

7. *Most people are good at heart.* The first response when things go wrong in groups is to look for someone to blame and punish. We often desire to vilify and demonize those we hold responsible for our problems. But very few people are totally hateful, mean, or evil. The vast majority of people are basically good, hard-working, honest folks.

8. *It's okay if you don't get your way.* We don't always get our way. Can you imagine if you got everything you ever wished for? You would be a gluttonous, wealthy, overindulged mess! We need to get beyond ourselves and begin to be aware of and responsive to the needs of those around us. We need to move from self to others. Don't get too hung up on what you want or what you desire. Learn to think of others too.

9. *It is better to face problems and responsibilities than avoid them.* It's irrational to avoid or deny actual problems or responsibilities facing you. Physical illness, relationship conflicts, and emotional distress need to be acknowledged and addressed. The same holds true for your responsibilities. You need to keep your promises, meet your legal obligations, and carry out your duties—especially when you work with others in groups, because the success of the group depends on each member taking responsibility to do his or her part.

10. *Let others be responsible for themselves.* It is irrational to be overly concerned about the lives of other people. We can be responsive to others, but not responsible for them. People need to live their own lives. There's an old saying, "Every time you help someone, you make them a little weaker, a little more dependent upon you." Let others be responsible for themselves.

These ten beliefs constitute a much more positive and healthy way of viewing yourself and others. You may find many of these beliefs helpful in talking to yourself in a more positive way. If you discover that an irrational belief is running through your mind and causing you some distress or pain, try to consciously hold the opposite belief in your mind and heart for an equal amount of time. Your words create what you become, so learn to speak more positively and kindly to yourself.

ACCEPTING YOURSELF

Even though you can invest a great deal of effort in increasing your self-awareness and speaking more kindly and positively to yourself, you can never come to a complete understanding of yourself. It's not possible in this lifetime, and I think a little mystery is good. What is important is that you take the time to ask yourself some questions about your life every once in a while: Who are you? What do you believe? What are your priorities? How do you communicate to others? What do you want to improve? What are you thankful for? The six inventories you completed in this chapter are invitations to self-discovery. Consider them as a way to stay in touch with yourself in the years to come.

> The worst loneliness is not to be comfortable with yourself.
> MARK TWAIN

Knowing yourself—having a sense of who and what you are—is important in your interactions with others in your small-group activities. Familiarity with yourself is essential before you enter into group work. You will be less apt to look to other group members for approval because you have already taken the time to examine and accept your strengths as well as your weaknesses. You will be more familiar with your skills, behavior, personality, and maybe even your soul. You will have attempted to accept the good with the bad. That is who you are, and no one's perfect.

I'm not suggesting you neglect or turn a blind eye to those areas you can improve or correct. Just the opposite. I'm suggesting you acknowledge and accept those things you can improve rather than deny or defend their existence. The first step in changing something is to accept its existence.

Self-acceptance means you don't have to be perfect. It's okay to have weaknesses—areas you want or need to improve. When you can acknowledge this in yourself, you are more likely to accept imperfection in others as well. Accepting others is the first step in working with them.

ACCEPTING OTHERS

We need to accept those who manners irritate us, whose ideas annoy us, and whose goals disturb us. Usually we try to distance ourselves from such individuals. We build walls or fences to keep them out, but in the end we cage ourselves in. More and more, we become prisoners of our own limited and ethnocentric view of the world, when in reality there are countless ways of seeing and experiencing life—ours being just one of the multitude.

The acceptance of others requires us to suspend judgment for a while. This doesn't mean we never evaluate, criticize, or blame. It means we silence our judging, condemning minds for a while and listen to others, even if their ideas are diametrically opposed to ours. It means we become more open to others—to broaden our definitions of what is acceptable, eligible, and tolerable. It means we overlook differences and seek similarities. It means we lighten up and open up to others.

Without this acceptance of others, our interactions in groups can be rigid, intolerant, and blaming. Our relationships with others can be marked by detachment, apathy, and even suspicion, except with those individuals who share our beliefs and goals. Without the acceptance of others, our commitment to the group and our participation in negotiation and compromise will be feeble and insecure. The acceptance of others is crucial to successful group work.

Successful group participation not only demands a basic understanding of group process; it also requires a level of self-knowledge. This chapter examined the idea of your being open to solitude and self-discovery. It looked at ways you can spend time by yourself and discussed the importance of accepting yourself and others in group communication. Now that you have had an opportunity to discover yourself a little more, you can create a more accepting, understanding, and compassionate atmosphere in your group work.

INDIVIDUAL AND GROUP EXERCISES

2.1 How Others See Your Communication Behavior

Have someone who knows you well, such as a family member, coworker, or friend, review your responses to Inventory 4 in this chapter. Briefly explain the inventory. Then have this person comment on your responses to each statement. Withhold judgment as you listen. Let the person talk about how he or she sees you and your communication behavior. Ask for suggestions on how to improve communication. Thank the person for sharing.

2.2 Communication Behaviors for You to Improve

Based on the responses you received in Exercise 2.1 and your own thoughtful consideration of your responses to Inventory 4, list three specific behaviors you would like to improve in the future. Before participating in any future group work or interpersonal interactions, remind yourself about these three behaviors. Make a conscious effort to improve them in the future.

2.3 Group Sharing of Individual Communication Behaviors

Make copies of Inventory 4 for group members you are currently working with. Ask group members to complete the inventory. When they have finished, make copies of each inventory and distribute them to group members. Distribute your inventory as well. One by one, have group members provide feedback to each member's inventory. This activity can prove very insightful in helping the group communicate more effectively.

CHAPTER THREE

Expressing Yourself Clearly

Speak your truth clearly
and kindly.

THOMAS MERTON

Every time Janet entered the conference room, the rest of us in the group would cringe, for we knew we would be in for a long evening.

Janet was one of nine members of an advisory board for a new teacher credential program at a local university, which met once a month to oversee this new program. Although the other members and I observed the usual norms of communication, Janet seemed to delight in breaking many of the rules. She would interrupt speakers in mid-sentence, criticize anyone who questioned an idea she had advanced, and scowl when others objected indirectly to her behavior.

What disturbed me most was Janet's controlling behavior. She would attempt to dominate the discussion with monologues supporting her position, misinterpret the remarks of others to fit her design, and challenge the chairperson with regularity. In short, Janet was a small group's nightmare.

During the sixth meeting, Janet conducted herself in her usual domineering manner and many of us offered subtle, and not so subtle, objections to her behavior. I felt sorry for her. Yet I realized her conduct was detrimental to the task and social dimensions of the group.

During our break I took a walk out to the parking lot to stretch my legs, and I saw Janet, in tears, hurrying to her car. I could hear her crying as she unlocked her car, not far from where I stood in the shadows of a building. Within a moment or so, I heard her engine roar as she sped out of the parking lot.

Apparently, during the break she and the chairperson had argued about her behavior, and Janet had resigned from the board right then and there. I was told Janet calmly strolled out of the room without uttering a word to any of the others in the group. That was the last they saw of her.

But I had seen Janet cry.

This chapter will explore the importance of communicating your thoughts and feelings effectively to others when you work in groups. Effective communication requires that you tell others what is on your mind while paying special attention to avoid dysfunctional ways of communicating, own your messages, understand gender differences in conversation strategies, and give feedback to others. If you learn to send clear messages, your messages will be received accurately and you can create more effective group interaction.

COMMUNICATION IS A LEARNED BEHAVIOR

I've often thought about Janet's tears in the parking lot that Tuesday night so many years ago. Her confident exterior, I thought, hid a troubled, perhaps lonely interior. Over the years I've been haunted by the image of her crying in her car. Did she treat her loved ones in the same controlling way? Were there any loved ones in her life? Had she always been this way? Where did she learn to be so pushy?

Janet, like you and me, learned most of her communication behavior in her family of origin. By the age of five, the fundamental structure of our personality has been established. Also by the age of five, the majority of our daily adult language has been learned and our basic communication patterns have been firmly established.

Can our communication patterns be changed? I believe they can. People can learn new ways of speaking, listening, and interacting with others. As a teacher, I have witnessed thousands of students improve the way they speak and listen. As a marriage and family counselor I have seen individuals and families correct dysfunctional patterns of interaction and replace them with more effective methods of communication. But change is not easy.

Most people are unaware of their own communication patterns and behavior. They often assume that communication skills are something they're born with—like breathing and blinking. They believe they are talking when their mouths are moving and they are listening when their mouths are shut. What could be simpler than that? However, you'll see that the communication process is actually more complex than you may first think. Let's begin by looking at communication roles that prevent you from expressing yourself clearly.

ROLES THAT PREVENT CLEAR EXPRESSION

Family therapist Virginia Satir has suggested four dysfunctional communication roles family members can adopt in their interactions with one another: computer, blamer, placater, and distractor. The computer is the cool, collected, intellectual family member who uses logic and reasoning as the primary method of communicating. The blamer is the family member who finds fault and casts blame on others. The placater is the peacemaker who tries to avoid or diffuse conflict at all costs by complying with the wishes of others. The distractor is the one who attempts to shift the focus off the conflict issue, using humor or irrelevant communication. This is a simplified explanation of Satir's communication roles, but it presents a valuable means for examining communication patterns.

> When old patterns are broken, new worlds emerge.
> TULI KUPFERBERG

I've constructed a modified version of Satir's model for groups: controller, blamer, pleaser, distractor, and ghost. As you examine these five roles and their characteristic patterns of behavior, you may recognize some aspects of yourself.

Controllers

Controllers try to dominate, regulate, and manipulate the interaction of the group. Their verbal communication patterns are usually issuing orders and directives. They tend to give directions and explain the superiority of their ideas and solutions over all others presented. Controllers often use logical appeals and intricate reasoning to get their way. They can be masters of words and persuasion. They block and redirect discussion for their own purposes. No matter what methodology they use, their ultimate goal is to control the group and achieve their objectives.

Blamers

Blamers usually find fault with others and their ideas and suggestions, but tend not to offer suggestions. They generally hold others accountable for the group's shortcomings and failures. Blamers cast a shadow of doubt and gloom on solutions the group proposes and are the first to say, "I told you so" when a solution fails.

Pleasers

Pleasers, similar to Satir's placaters, attempt to avoid all conflict and confrontation by giving in to the wishes of the others. They agree to just about anything the others ask or require. When a conflict begins to arise, pleasers do whatever it takes to dissolve or neutralize the disagreement. They are generally uncomfortable asserting opinions, defending positions, and sharing feelings. Pleasers back down rather than fight. They agree to just about anything for the sake of peace and tranquility.

Distractors

Rather than give in, blame, or control, **distractors** draw or deflect attention away from the issue at hand. When the group experiences stress or conflict, distractors usually joke about the situation or redirect the discussion to an unrelated issue or topic. Oftentimes distractors are just as uncomfortable with conflict as pleasers, but their method for handling discomfort is different. Whereas pleasers placate or give in, distractors utilize some avoidance technique to change the subject. They will joke, flirt, or question the importance of tasks. They are often the court jester, the class clown.

Ghosts

Ghosts are individuals who don't participate in discussions or just don't show up. Just as the word suggests, participation of ghosts is nonexistent. Like a silent face in the crowd, ghosts sit in the group and say nothing or don't even show up. The cause of this behavior may be stage fright, lack of commitment, apathy, or a host of other explanations, but the result is always the same—nonparticipation or absence. Ghosts are often labeled the nonperformer, the low-verbal, and the passive-aggressive personality; I simply refer to them as ghosts because they are not really there to contribute to the group's efforts.

Do any of these role descriptions sound or feel familiar to you? Do they remind you of someone from your family of origin? A friend or coworker? More important, do you see yourself in any of these five dysfunctional communication roles? If so, you may want to explore your reasons for these behaviors and consider modifying or eliminating them if they no longer serve a purpose in your life.

These five basic dysfunctional roles will appear from time to time during your work with others in groups. Your awareness and ability to recognize these roles will greatly enhance your understanding and effectiveness in your small-group work.

THE COMMUNICATION PROCESS

Very few people would welcome the thought of living the rest of their lives in complete isolation from other humans. The prospect of spending life alone on a desert island or facing the horrors of solitary confinement would be intolerable for many of us. The purpose of life is found in our relationships with others. The primary way we initiate, develop, and maintain these relationships is through the communication process. **Communication** is a transactional process in which communicators attempt to influence others and are influenced by others. **Communicators** are the individuals who send and receive messages simultaneously from one another during the communication event. A **message** is the thought or feeling a communicator wants to convey. It's the give and take of life itself.

The communication process operates in two forms—verbal and nonverbal communication.

Verbal Communication

Verbal communication is all spoken and written communication. These are the words of communication, whether they are being boisterously delivered in a speech or silently read in a book. From the moment you vocalize your first word as a toddler to the last words you utter on your deathbed, your verbal communication is essential to your efforts to live your life.

When you work in groups, keep in mind four principles of verbal communication—it is symbolic; it is rule governed; it defines and limits; and it lets us create. Verbal communication is symbolic in that words stand for or represent things in the real world. They are not the actual things they represent. Verbal communication is rule governed because syntactic rules prescribe the order of words in a sentence. For instance, "I am turning off the computer" is syntactically correct, whereas "Off the am I turning computer" doesn't make much sense.

Verbal communication defines and limits. Language is used to define things, which also limits the thing being defined. For instance, if I said that Lisa is an ineffective manager, I have defined her as a manager and limited her to the status of ineffective as opposed to outstanding, effective, or satisfactory. Finally, verbal communication lets us create. You can arrange the thousands upon thousands of words contained in the English language in an endless variety of combinations and structures to communicate your thoughts and feelings. Different combinations of words enable you to express a message in a way that reflects your attitude, mood, and personality. This is one of the joys of life—to create messages that are uniquely yours.

Nonverbal Communication

Nonverbal communication is all communication that is not spoken or written. Nonverbal communication comes in a myriad of forms and is delivered in immeasurable ways. It's embedded in the clothes you wear, the tone of your voice, the posture you present, the gestures you use, the facial expressions you flash, or the car you drive. It's your silence, your gentle touch, your downcast eyes, or your deep, relaxed breathing. All these things and countless others constitute nonverbal communication behavior.

Although we spend a great deal of our formal education learning to communicate verbally with others through reading, writing, and sometimes even speaking, we rarely receive any specific coaching or training in nonverbal communication. The entire universe of nonverbal messages above, below, around, and through the verbal messages is usually neglected in formal education, yet researchers have been telling us for years that nonverbal communication can have more impact on us than verbal messages in many situations.

> What you are stands over you the while, and thunders so that I cannot hear what you say to the contrary.
>
> RALPH WALDO EMERSON

When you work in groups, keep in mind the following principles of nonverbal communication—it is continuous; it conveys emotions; it is more universal than verbal communication; it is multichanneled; and it is ambiguous. Nonverbal communication is continuous and always present. Whereas a sentence ends and talking stops, your body posture, your facial expressions, and your clothing can communicate messages long after you have stopped speaking. Nonverbal communication conveys emotions much more effectively and quickly than verbal communication. Your facial expressions, tone of voice, and posture can communicate your feelings of tenderness, anger, frustration, or joy much faster and more profoundly than words could ever accomplish.

Nonverbal communication is also more universal than verbal language. Emotions such as anger, sadness, joy, surprise, and boredom can be communicated to others by your facial expressions and body language, regardless of language barriers or cultural differences. Nonverbal communication is also multichanneled in that messages can be sent in all five sensory channels, whereas most verbal communication must flow through auditory and visual channels. Finally, nonverbal communication is ambiguous. By that I mean that it really is impossible to "read someone like a book." Nonverbal communication is far too complex and difficult to interpret to convey any one specific message or meaning to a given behavior or act. Someone's folded arms during a business meeting can be interpreted in a variety of ways. The person could be cold, bored, comfortable, defensive, angry, or hiding a food stain from lunch. One thing you can do when nonverbal communication is ambiguous is to ask questions. Rather than guess at the meaning of a particular behavior or act, you can always ask the other person and open up the lines of communication.

The Transactional Nature of Communication

By using the verbal and nonverbal forms of expression, we participate in the most important activity there is—communication. Communication is **transactional**; that is, each person communicating is simultaneously sending *and* receiving messages and has an interdependent influence or impact on the other. In other words, by interacting, you affect the other communicator and, in turn, you are affected by him or her. There is a constant give and take that occurs throughout the transactional communication processes, as shown in the figure.

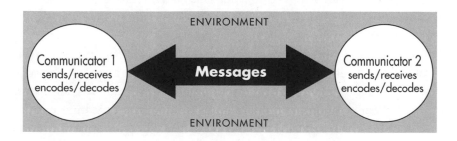

A communicator must **encode** or convert a message into verbal and nonverbal symbols that others will understand. The encoding process is highly complex. The words selected, the rate of speech, the tone of voice, facial expressions, and body language are determined by the source communicator's relationship with the receiver, purpose, speaking situation, and countless other variables. The **decoding** process involves making sense out of messages. The receiving communicator must decipher the words and the nonverbal cues sent by the other person so they have meaning for him or her. **Noise** is any physical or psychological interference that reduces the accurate decoding of a message, such as the sound of ambient talking, a jackhammer nearby, or multiple meanings for a given work. After decoding the message, the receiving communicator encodes a return message and sends it on its way.

The most important aspect to remember about these encoding and decoding processes is that they occur simultaneously within each communicator. As one individual is formulating a sentence to express a thought or feeling (encoding), he or she is *simultaneously* observing and trying to make sense (decoding) of the nonverbal behaviors or feedback from the other communicator. Effective communicators will read the feedback accurately and adjust their messages appropriately. In this sense, the process of communication is transactional; each communicator influences and is influenced by the other communicator.

In addition to the mutual impact of the communicators, the channel, background, and environment influence the communication act. A **channel** is the medium by which the message is communicated. A communicator can utilize the channels of sound, sight, smell, touch, and taste to send a message. For instance, you can utilize a variety of channels or combinations of channels to communicate affection to another person. You can say, "I like you" (sound). You can wink your eye (sight). You can hug the individual (touch). You can send some cookies (taste) you baked to the person. Or you can send a bottle of perfume (smell). Usually, the more channels you utilize, the more impact your message will have on the receiver.

The encoding and decoding processes of both communicators is influenced by their individual **backgrounds**. Communicators' personal histories, personalities, genders, races, ages, knowledge, experiences, attitudes, beliefs, and emotions influence their communication experience. It determines to a great extent how they will encode and decode messages during the communication process. In addition to the personal backgrounds of the communicators, the **environment** or context of the communication setting affects and influences the communicators and how they process the communication interaction. The physical surroundings, the specific occasion within which the communication occurs, the noise level, the temperature, and the interruptions from machines and people all influence the communication process.

The most important thing to keep in mind as you communicate with others in groups is that what you choose to say and how you choose to behave will have an impact on the other group members. It affects not only how they modify and readjust their messages to you, but also their behaviors. In the transactional model of communication, your words and behaviors can influence others and how well you work together.

I-STATEMENTS

I-statements are the first step in communicating clear messages. By using I-statement language to encode a message, you take ownership of your thoughts and feelings. Here are some examples of simple I-statements:

> *I* believe trucks are the most useful vehicles.
> *I* think education is important to personal growth.
> *I* feel upset by what I heard at this morning's meeting.
> It's *my* opinion that you are correct.

Do you notice how the speaker takes ownership of the opinion or feeling expressed? Do you also notice how an I-statement doesn't necessarily have to contain the word *I* to qualify as an I-statement? For example, "It's *my* opinion that you're correct" shows ownership ("my") even though it doesn't contain the word *I*.

I-statements provide several advantages. First, when a speaker uses I-statements, the listener of the message knows who the originator or owner of the statement is. If I-statements are not used, the ownership of the message is often uncertain or overstated.

A second advantage to I-statements is that they provide a target for the listener of the message to respond. If a speaker says, *"Everyone thinks the 49ers are the best team,"* the listener might be less likely to disagree, because the speaker uses the word *everyone* as the source of the message. At a subconscious level, it might be difficult to confront or argue with "everyone" rather than with an individual.

A third advantage to I-statements is that they let you know when people are speaking for others. For instance, the statement "My wife likes to go camping" shows the husband is speaking for the wife.

A fourth advantage to I-statements is that they are more thoughtful statements. Because they show ownership, I-statements force speakers to weigh their remarks more cautiously. I think (I-statement) it's easier to flippantly say, "*Everyone* really likes you," rather than owning the statement and saying, "*I* like you."

A final advantage to I-statements is that they help prevent blaming others. Many times a speaker uses what is called "you-language" instead of I-statements. The speaker sends "you" messages such as "*You* make me mad" and "*You*'re a grouch," directing blame to the listener of the message. If the speaker were to use I-statements such as "*I* get mad when you call me lazy" or "*I* notice you're not smiling," the tone of the statement is less blaming and fault-finding. Ownership of thoughts and feelings through I-statements enables you to communicate more effectively with your group.

FOUR LEVELS OF COMMUNICATION

There are four levels of communication—surface talk, reporting facts, giving opinions, and sharing feelings. Each level of communication shares a different degree of information. **Surface talk** merely acknowledges others without really sharing. **Reporting facts** shares information that can be verified or proven. **Giving opinions** provides personal views, attitudes, and beliefs. **Sharing feelings** involves the most intimate information—our feelings and emotions. You are not restricted to communicating at just one level. You can communicate from all four levels of disclosure during the course of one conversation.

Level 1: Surface Talk

In this first level of sharing, we keep conversations to a minimal level of disclosure. The surface-talk level of sharing includes greetings, casual acknowledgment of strangers and acquaintances, chitchat with a coworker, and so on. The primary goal is to acknowledge another human being without having to provide any personal information about ourselves. Listen to the following surface-level remarks:

How's it going? / Fine. How about you? / Fine.
Looks like rain. / Maybe.
Have a good day. / You, too. / Thanks.

As you can see, there isn't any real disclosure going on in these statements. Their purpose isn't to conduct a deep, involved conversation. Both parties are merely acknowledging each other in a socially acceptable fashion.

Surface talk is just another way of saying, "I see you and I want to acknowledge you," and usually nothing more. It's a way of being polite to people we come in contact with. It would be humanly impossible to conduct in-depth discussions with everyone we saw in a given day. We probably wouldn't want to, anyway.

Level 2: Reporting Facts

The second level of communicating involves the reporting of facts. Reporting the outside temperature, giving directions to a stranger, demonstrating how to tune a carburetor, giving a lecture on the mating habits of moths, providing information about a car you're selling through the papers, and answering questions during an interview are examples of reporting factual information.

Facts are different from opinions in that they can be verified. A thermometer can verify the temperature. A map can verify the directions you're giving. A car manual can verify your directions on tuning a carburetor. Scientific research can verify the information in your lecture. Your tune-up receipts can verify your statements about the car's maintenance history. Your previous employers can verify your information regarding past employment performance. The key to identifying communication at this level is that the content of the messages can be verified or proven. The following statements report facts:

I weigh 162 pounds.
I was employed by Apple Computer from 1998 to 2000.
It rained two inches in San Francisco during December.

At the reporting-fact level, there isn't usually a great deal of personal information being shared. Sure, there could be exceptions, such as, "I've been in a mental hospital for twenty years," but the majority of factual information reveals little about your opinions or feelings.

Level 3: Giving Opinions

Giving opinions is a little more risky than surface talk or reporting facts. By giving your opinions about topics, people, or events, you are exposing more of who you are. You are allowing others to see more of you by sharing your opinions, attitudes, and beliefs with them. This level is much more threatening because there is a greater chance of disagreement, disapproval, and conflict brought about by opinion differences with others.

But disagreement is natural. We couldn't possibly agree on every topic we discuss with others. And we wouldn't want to. That's the beauty of life. It's often our differences that make people interesting to us. They complement our weaknesses and show us new ways of seeing, thinking, and feeling. The following statements give opinions:

It's my *opinion* gun control would not lower violent crime.

I *know* this plan will work.

I *believe* if we go to counseling, we'll continue our relationship.

Level 4: Sharing Feelings

The deepest level of communication is the sharing of feelings. It's at this level two people really communicate for connection—the feeling level. Sharing feelings can be extremely beneficial in your communication with a small group because it directly invites discussion about the social dimension of the group. Many difficulties experienced in the social dimension of the group could be avoided if individuals would be more willing to share their feelings before anger, resentment, or hurt got in the way of effective communication.

Here is a list of feeling words to get you in the mood. This feeling list can provide you with a richer look at the emotional world in which you live. Have fun!

accepted	edgy	intense	restless
afraid	elated	intimidated	sad
annoyed	embarrassed	irritable	sensual
anxious	enthusiastic	jazzed	sentimental
ashamed	ecstatic	joyful	shaky
bashful	excited	lonely	shy
bewildered	fearful	moving	silly
bitter	foolish	mean	strong

bored	free	miserable	subdued
brave	frustrated	needed	tender
calm	furious	neglected	tense
confident	glum	nervous	terrified

Sharing feelings is the most intimate way you can verbally connect with others. It provides others with information about your heart—your joy, your fear, your anger, and your love. Without this information, we are merely two-dimensional stick figures who never reveal the deeper dimensions of who we are.

GENDER DIFFERENCES IN CONVERSATIONAL STRATEGIES

During your life, you have most likely observed different conversational styles for men and women. Not surprisingly, numerous communication researchers have discovered differences in the conversational strategies used by men and women. Linguistics professor Deborah Tannen, in her book *You Just Don't Understand,* states that "communication between men and women can be like cross-cultural communication, falling prey to a clash of conversational styles." It is not so much that men and women desire to be in conflict with one another; it's just that their conversational strategies are so different. Tannen adds that "women speak and hear a language of connection and intimacy, while men speak and hear a language of status and independence." These are of course generalizations, and you should keep in mind that there are many exceptions. Additional differences can be attributed to age, culture, economic background, education level, and so forth. For our purposes, we will focus our attention on the gender differences in communication strategies.

Men seem to use more competitive strategies, whereas women use more cooperative strategies. This difference can be the source of misunderstanding and conflict. Tannen further clarifies these conversational style differences by making the distinction between symmetrical and asymmetrical relationships.

A **symmetrical relationship** is one that is characterized by cooperation, equality, rapport building, acceptance, listening, questioning, empathy, exploring problems, encouragement, mutual understanding, complimenting, and negotiating. Tannen's research indicates that women most often demonstrate these behaviors in their conversational strategies, which encourage and maintain connection and a sense of community. Women tend to invest effort in establishing rapport, asking questions, listening without interrupting, being supportive, agreeing, complimenting, and sharing feelings. Their focus is more on the quality of relationship, rather than problem solving or competing with others. The symmetrical relationship is one of equality, connection, and cooperation.

The asymmetrical relationship is characterized by lecturing, giving advice, directing, commanding, evaluating, problem-solving, challenging, and competing. Tannen believes that men most typify these communication behaviors in their conversational strategies. Men tend to report facts and information, lecture, use more commanding language, ask fewer questions, interrupt, give advice, evaluate, challenge, and problem-solve. The focus is more on reporting, lecturing, fixing, and competing.

The relationship between the speakers in an asymmetrical conversation is secondary to the task at hand or the subject being discussed. In fact, competition characterizes much of the male conversational strategies, in which the desire to know, to be right, and to win is foremost in their minds. The asymmetrical relationship is brought about by the competitive nature of the male conversational strategies because there is often a constant jockeying for the top position, the endless struggle to win in this competitive activity of talking.

> To become fully human, we must learn to develop the other parts of ourselves.
>
> CARL JUNG

How can all this information help you in your small-group work? Plenty! You can become aware of and appreciate these differences in conversational strategies between men and women. Rather than blame, punish, or withdraw from a disagreement or argument brought about by differences in conversational strategies, you might be able to establish new lines of communication. Here are some suggestions you might consider as you attempt to create new ways of talking and listening:

Men

Put the newspaper down when someone is talking.
Listen without interrupting, judging, or fixing.

Ask open-ended questions (How? Why? What?).

Paraphrase to prove understanding ("Are you saying . . . ?").

Communicate agreement ("I agree . . . ," "I see your point . . . ," "You've got a valid point . . .").

Communicate empathy ("That must have felt . . . ," "I know how you feel . . .").

Encourage exploration ("What else . . . ?" "How else . . . ?" "How did that feel?").

Compliment ("I appreciate your . . . ," "I like your . . . ," "I admire the way you . . .").

Negotiate ("How can we . . . ?" "What other solutions . . . ?" "Can we live with . . . ?").

Share your perceptions (especially strengths) about your relationships.

Share your feelings.

Listen *again,* without interrupting, judging, or fixing.

Women

State your opinions more often ("I think . . . ," "I believe . . . ," "It's my opinion that . . .").

Label a transaction when interrupted ("May I speak?" "You're interrupting me.").

Label a transaction when being lectured ("I believe you're lecturing me.").

Invite your own participation ("Would you like to hear my opinion/feeling?" "I want to share my opinion/ feeling.").

Disagree ("I'm not convinced." "I have a different opinion." "I see it differently." "This is what I think . . .").

State a need ("May I state a need?" "I need . . .").

State a boundary ("No, that's not okay with me." "This is unacceptable.").

State a boundary with consequence ("If you continue to . . . , then I'm prepared to . . .").

Give advice ("I think you should . . . ," "You might consider . . . ," "What if you . . .").

Give a command ("I want you to . . . ," "Please get me . . . ," "Don't say . . . ," "Don't do . . .").

These suggested communication behaviors can be used to provide you with different conversational strategies than you might be accustomed to using in your group work. The goal is to expand the use of all the communication options available so you can exercise more creativity as you interact with others.

GUIDELINES FOR EXPRESSING YOURSELF CLEARLY

When you are working with others, how you communicate directly affects your group's interactions and success. Keep in mind these guidelines for expressing yourself clearly.

Be Specific, Not Vague

When speaking, try to use specific language. A common mistake is to assume the listener will visualize the same picture that you have when you say a word. When I say, "I see a dog," you hear my sentence and decode the meaning of my words. The word *dog* is a relatively abstract, vague term. The dog you "see" in your head could be big, small, shaggy, or short-haired. You could "see" a bulldog, a collie, or a mutt. What I saw in my mind, and intended to communicate, was a German shepherd. Notice the difference between your picture and mine?

Use specific language to communicate what you think and feel to others. It will prevent a great deal of misunderstanding in your interactions with others.

Communicate Observations, Not Inferences

Observations refer to what your five senses have gathered: what you have seen with your eyes, heard with your ears, smelled with your nose, felt with your fingers, and tasted with your tongue. Inferences, on the other hand, go beyond what you have observed and make assumptions about what you think and feel. Notice the difference between the following observation and inference statements:

> The two people are walking arm in arm. (observation)
> That couple is in love. (inference)

Communicate about a Behavior, Not the Person

It's important to communicate about people's behavior, rather than comment on what you think they are like. Use adverbs (relating to actions) to describe people rather than adjectives (relating to qualities). Communicating in this way is more specific because you report behaviors rather than attempt to label the person. Notice the difference in the following statements:

> Harvey has been talking for ten minutes. (describes behavior)
> Harvey is a loudmouth. (describes person)

Communicate in Terms of "More or Less," Not "Either-Or"

We tend to use polar terms when communicating with others. It was either the most wonderful event or the worst event. Either the person was smart or the person was stupid. Our laziness often displays itself in our communication. Rather than force descriptions of people, places, and things into extreme terminology with "either-or" language, try to communicate in terms of degree ("more or less" language). For example, rather than saying, "Pat is the loudest person on earth" (either loudest or softest), you could restate your opinion: "Pat speaks louder than Chris" (matter of degree).

Share Ideas, Not Advice

Avoid the tendency to evaluate and give advice to others. Rather, communicate the sharing of ideas and alternatives instead of giving advice and solutions. For example, instead of saying, "You should get a divorce" (advice), you could suggest, "There are a number of things you can do to improve your marriage, such as take a vacation, enroll in a communication class, or enter into therapy" (suggesting options). This approach lets the other person consider and decide. It also allows the person to save face rather than be proven wrong and be instructed by you.

Communicate What Was Said, Not Why It Was Said

Try not to assess motive or reasoning behind what another person says. Instead of getting into the area of inference and assumption, focus your communication on observable information introduced by such words as *what, how, when,* and *where.* This will keep the discussion on a level that is more effectively communicated and debated, rather than entering into the domain of motive and assumption.

Match Nonverbal and Verbal Communication

When speaking, try to match your voice, body, and gestures with the content of your verbal message. Mixed messages—inconsistent nonverbal and verbal messages—confuse the listener and threaten clear communication. When you say, "I enjoy spending time with you," your face, voice, and body should also communicate the same message with a smile, a cheerful voice, and a relaxed and open body posture.

Keep these seven suggestions for clear communication in mind when you work in groups. You will discover that your communication, as well as your thinking, will be more specific, congruent, and collaborative.

Your ability and willingness to send clear messages when you interact with others is essential to making groups work effectively. To own your statements and share information, opinions, and feelings in specific, nonthreatening ways will enable you to communicate clearly and invite others to share more openly with you. Use these skills to create successful group interaction.

INDIVIDUAL AND GROUP EXERCISES

3.1 Family of Origin Communication Roles

Think back to your family of origin and see if you can identify who may have played the roles of controller, blamer, pleaser, distractor, or ghost during times of stress or crisis. Identifying family members and their roles is not meant to blame them, but to discover patterns of behavior—theirs and yours. Write their name(s) beside the dysfunctional communication role.

1. Controller: _____
2. Blamer: _____
3. Pleaser: _____
4. Distractor: _____
5. Ghost: _____

Did your family members fit any of the dysfunctional communication roles? Did some play more than one role? What, if any, role(s) did you play within the family? Do family members still play these roles?

One important discovery you can make is the role you played (or still play) in your family of origin. Because if you did, there's a good chance you play a similar role when working in groups. A controller in the family will often try to control others in groups. Likewise, a pleaser in the family will often try to please others outside the family. Be aware of the roles you play when you communicate with others.

3.2 Making I-Statements to Two People

The disclosure of your thoughts and feelings is important for others in their attempts to work with and understand you. It is even more important for you to get a sense of who you are. You achieve this sense of self-intimacy, paradoxically, by sharing your thoughts and feelings with others, not by holding them in or hiding them from the listening ear of others.

List two individuals from your personal or professional life to whom you would like to communicate a thought or feeling, but haven't had the courage or the opportunity to do so with yet. These can be positive or negative thoughts or feelings. Write the names of the persons and then briefly note what you would share with them (one sentence only).

How did you feel writing these thoughts or feelings down? What do you think or feel as you see these messages on the page before you? Would you ever consider sharing these messages with the people you listed? If yes, when will you share with them?

3.3 Group Role-Play

Have your group make plans for a hypothetical group vacation. Determine where the group will go, how long you will stay, and how much money you will need. Decide what rules will be observed for fun and safety. Finally, select a vacation theme.

As the group discusses this topic, have each member role-play one of the five dysfunctional roles: controller, blamer, pleaser, distractor, and ghost. As you talk, stay in your role. If you have more than five group members, have the remaining people role-play themselves. After three minutes of discussion, switch roles and resume talking. Continue to switch dysfunctional roles every three minutes, until all the discussion questions are answered.

Discuss what it felt like to play these different roles. Was there a role you felt uncomfortable playing? Was there a role you felt comfortable playing? How did it feel to interact with others when they were playing their roles? How did the role-playing affect the discussion? What did you learn from this experience?

→ Goal to understand behavorial roles.

CHAPTER FOUR

Listening for Understanding

No one can develop fully without feeling
understood by at least one person.

PAUL TOURNIER

THE OAK LOG CRACKLES AND SNAPS in the fireplace as the orange flames dance softly above the wood. I stare into the fire, feeling its heat on my face and hands. We both sit silently in overstuffed chairs, while an occasional red ember shoots out from the fire and bounces onto the stone floor in front of us.

Being here in this small, rustic cottage feels good to me. The warm, golden glow from two kerosene lanterns and the sound of the crackling fire soothe me as a light winter rain falls outside. But what feels best is the way Winston listens to me.

Winston has been my friend and mentor now for twenty years. I trust his counsel. I appreciate his friendship. But most of all, I like being heard by him—to be understood at the deepest level.

I've come to this cottage to talk to Winston. Or, rather, to be heard by him. You see, Winston has that rare ability to listen for understanding—to listen without interruption, evaluation, or advice. When Winston senses I need to be heard, he listens with an acceptance of who I am—not what he wants me to be.

When he listens to understand, I can hear myself think. He doesn't interrupt my story with his story. He doesn't pass judgment, offer criticism, or give advice. He won't even try to rescue, teach, or assist. Winston simply sits and listens in silence. When he does speak, he'll ask a question. His questions invite me to explore and discover; not defend, justify, or even explain. Like a mirror, he lets me see myself, and I am better because of it. I'm a better husband, father, teacher, and therapist because he has listened for understanding.

This chapter will explore the skill of listening for understanding. Your ability to listen and understand what other people in your group are saying will directly determine the success of your interactions with them. Without your ability and willingness to suspend judgment long enough to really hear what others are attempting to communicate, you will forever be destined to hear only the echoes of your own thinking and evaluation. The ability to listen for understanding creates the foundation for an effective group.

THE IMPORTANCE OF LISTENING

According to an old saying, "We were given two ears and only one mouth, so that we might hear more than we speak." Can you imagine having it the other way around, attempting to communicate with only one ear and two mouths? The possibilities are humorous, and even a little frightening. Yet the attitudes and the behavior we often carry into our discussions reflect exactly that—trying to talk more and listen less. In the U.S. culture, talking is valued much more than listening. The individual who is articulate, persuasive, and even inspirational while addressing the group is often regarded as influential and powerful.

Yet that makes sense, you may be saying to yourself. Speaking is important. We can't be successful without developing this skill. But listening is just as important. In fact, it may be more important than speaking. Studies show that we spend 45 percent of our communication time each day listening, and only 30 percent speaking, 16 percent reading, and 9 percent writing. To make matters worse, studies also suggest that we remember

> Take a tip from nature,
> your ears aren't made to shut,
> but your mouth is.
> MALCOLM FORBES

only 25 percent of what we hear after two days. Listening is important, but we don't do it very well.

During our communication in groups, we probably don't even realize that our listening isn't very effective. Often we don't listen to others in ways that encourage them to disclose more about themselves. Instead, we get in their way, we switch the discussion to our point of view, and the opportunity for them to speak is often lost. How can we improve our listening?

THE PROCESS OF LISTENING

Many of us think that listening comes as naturally as breathing, but it requires much more attention and skill than just keeping quiet while someone else speaks. **Listening** is the process of receiving, attending, understanding, responding, and remembering. The first step in the listening process is **receiving**, or hearing sounds from your environment. Hearing is limited to the physiological process of receiving and processing the sounds. The second step is **attending**, which is the process of paying attention to some of the sounds you receive and disregarding or filtering out the others. For instance, you may hear a number of individuals talking at the same time during a discussion, but you attend to or single out only one individual. **Understanding**, the third step, involves comprehending the message. The fourth step, **responding**, includes asking questions or giving feedback to the speaker. The final step in the listening process is **remembering** what was said. As you can see, listening requires your active participation.

POOR LISTENING STYLES

Our poor listening habits often prevent others from opening up to us. We give the impression we are listening when in fact we are daydreaming, arranging our rebuttals, or changing the subject to accommodate our interests. Four styles of listening to avoid when you are trying to be receptive to another person are refusing to listen, pseudolistening, listening selectively, and listening to evaluate.

Refusing to Listen

The most obvious behavior that prevents effective listening is to refuse to listen to the other person. Here are some examples of refusing to listen:

> simply walking away when someone begins speaking
> I've had enough. I don't want to talk about this anymore.
> I don't want to hear what you have to say.

Pseudolistening

Pretending to listen, or **pseudolistening**, is the second poor listening style to avoid. In this style, listeners demonstrate many of the nonverbal behaviors of true listening—an open posture, eye contact, nodding, and appropriate facial expressions—but make no attempt to receive, attend, or understand the content of what the speaker is saying. Here are some comments that suggest pseudolistening:

> You bet, I got the message.
> Okay, dear.
> Whatever.
> Ah hum . . .

Listening Selectively

Often listeners attend and respond only to those subjects that interest them and skip the rest. We've all endured individuals who listen to us just long enough to bring up a topic they're interested in and then dominate the conversation. Here are some statements that suggest listening selectively:

> That reminds me of a time when I . . .
> Now you're talking about something I'm interested in.
> I'm glad you finally brought that up because I had that happen
>   to me . . .

Listening to Evaluate

Rather than hear and try to understand the speaker's opinions, feelings, and frame of reference, listeners can be primarily focused on judging the message from their own point of view. Listening to evaluate focuses on judging the correctness, rightness, or worth of the speaker's statements. It doesn't matter whether a listener's evaluation is negative or positive; the goal is to judge what the speaker is saying. Whether the response is "That's a wonderful point!" or "That's the most ridiculous opinion I've ever heard!" the listener's deeper message is "I am the judge of your comments." Listening for the purposes of judging does not encourage or provide a basis of understanding. Here are some responses that suggest listening for judgment:

> That's a good point. I agree.
> No one should say that.
> You're wrong. How can you say that?

There might be occasions when using one of these four listening styles is appropriate. But if your primary purpose for listening is to create an open atmosphere in your group discussions, then avoid them.

BARRIERS TO LISTENING

In addition to avoiding poor listening styles, there are five specific barriers to listening that you need to be aware of if you are to be an effective listener. The first barrier is the **overabundance** of messages that bombard us every day, messages crying out to be heard and listened to—the sounds of radio, television, endless conversations, business meetings, phone messages, and phone conversations. The list goes on and on. There are just too many things to listen to in our lives.

External noise, or interference from outside sources, is the second barrier to listening. Some examples of external noise are traffic, barking dogs, machinery, and the music from our neighbor's stereo. These external noises make listening difficult.

> Man's inability to communicate is a result of his failure to listen effectively, skillfully, and with understanding to another human being.
>
> CARL ROGERS

Our **rapid thought** is the third barrier to listening. We can understand a person's speech up to 500 words per minute, whereas the average person speaks about 125 words per minute. With all this spare time on our hands, our thoughts can drift—we can think about our response to what is being said or just daydream about food.

The fourth barrier to listening is our **preoccupation with self**. We think in terms of how communication affects us, what it means to us, and whether it agrees or disagrees with what we think, feel, and believe. We focus on what we think, feel, and believe, and it is through this filter that we listen to what others say.

The final barrier to effective listening is **effort**. Effective listening demands that we pay attention, process what is being said, and interact appropriately.

Listening for understanding requires that we put aside our ego, pay attention to what is being shared, ask questions to clarify the messages, and respond in ways that demonstrate understanding. More than anything else, listening requires our acceptance of others.

ACCEPTANCE—A REQUIREMENT FOR LISTENING

Acceptance can be defined as "receiving what is." The basis of all listening is acceptance—to be open to receive whatever it is that the speaker is sharing with us. No receptive listening can occur without being open to the other person.

When it comes to listening to others, we often feel the urge to judge, fix, blame, control, help, criticize, or rescue them, rather than accept what they have to share. These urges surface most noticeably in our listening habits. Instead of listening in silence with an open mind, ready to receive "what is," we judge, blame, criticize, tell our story, or give advice. We are rarely open and receptive to what the speaker wants to share.

We must be willing to listen to different ideas, thoughts, and feelings when we listen to others, or forever be at odds with them, ourselves, and the world. By being more open-minded and receptive to what others in your group have to say, you will be creating an atmosphere in which more open-minded and receptive communication is encouraged. You can communicate acceptance both nonverbally and verbally.

Noverbal Signs of Acceptance

Would it be easy for you to hold a conversation with an individual who frowns and looks away every time you try to speak? Can you imagine what it would be like to talk and have that person respond with labored sighs of disgust and disapproval? Not a pretty sight. Nonverbal behavior sets the tone of acceptance or rejection long before you speak. The manner in which you make yourself available to another person by your posture and gestures, eye contact, facial expressions, and nodding demonstrates your acceptance of them.

Posture and gestures. How you stand or sit can communicate acceptance or rejection. Facing away from a person or speaking over your shoulder can communicate rejection, whereas facing the person directly can communicate more acceptance. When you are seated, your slouched, withdrawn posture can communicate negative messages, whereas your erect posture or one in which you lean toward the person can communicate more positive messages. Your arms and hands can also be a source of acceptance by being open, rather than being crossed or placed over your ears.

Eye contact. Eye contact can communicate acceptance in the American culture. It can be a sign of acknowledgment, approval, and agreement, especially when accompanied by a smile. To refuse to look at someone can be interpreted as a sign of rejection. When you are listening, your eye contact should be direct. Maintain eye contact with the speaker to demonstrate your interest and involvement. Don't look away or close your eyes and fall asleep. Look at the speaker for three or four seconds at a time. Don't stare for long periods of time, however. Staring can make others feel uncomfortable, so maintain direct eye contact for short periods. When interacting with individuals from other cultures, be as sensitive as possible to their norms and expectations; for example, direct eye contact can be regarded as impolite or rude in many Asian cultures.

Facial expressions. Your face can communicate a great deal about how you are feeling and what you are thinking. A frown, raised eyebrows, and rolling eyes are just a few facial expressions that can convey your thoughts and feelings. So, if you are trying to communicate acceptance, remember to reflect the appropriate facial expressions when someone speaks. Supportive facial expressions help to create a sense of acceptance.

Nodding. You can communicate acknowledgment by nodding. An occasional nod is an encouraging nonverbal message that says you are paying attention and acknowledging the words of the speaker. Don't overdo this behavior, but use it as a way of saying, "I hear you" and "What you're saying is important."

Verbal Signs of Acceptance

There are a number of verbal ways to communicate your acceptance while listening. These verbal signs of acceptance are not interrupting, nonevaluative listening, verbal responses of acceptance, and invitations to share.

Not interrupting. Two people cannot speak at the same time and expect communication to occur. Whenever someone speaks, someone else needs to listen. So your willingness to listen sends a very important message. Instead of interrupting or adding your own comments every twelve to fifteen seconds, let the speaker talk nonstop for thirty to sixty seconds. In some instances, it may be beneficial for you to remain silent for a minute or two.

Nonevaluative listening. By withholding your evaluation or judgment as the speaker talks, you are listening nonevaluatively. Many people are inclined to evaluate everything that is being shared. Like a judge, they listen with gavel in hand, ready to pronounce judgment even before the speaker has finished his or her sentence. Don't interrupt with opinions or advice. Just keep silent and listen, offering only supportive nonverbal responses.

Verbal responses of acceptance. Verbal responses of acceptance include words or phrases such as "Oh," "Um," "Really?" "Okay," "I see," "Is that so?" "That's interesting," and "Say more." These responses are not evaluations of right or wrong, good or bad, or agreement or disagreement. They are intended to communicate your attentiveness and your acceptance of what is being shared. It is your way to cheer the speaker on and say, "Keep going, you're doing a great job sharing!"

Invitations to share. You can invite others to share by issuing invitations such as "How is it going?" This invitation is neutral and gives people the choice to talk or to decline. However people respond to your invitation, honor their decision. If they decide to talk, listen nonevaluatively. If they decline, accept that also. What's important is that you are inviting them to share. You are creating the opportunity for them to talk. Other invitations to share are:

> Share your thoughts with me.
> Tell me about it.
> I'm interested in your point of view.

These are just a few ways you can encourage someone to open up. Your invitations to share can create an atmosphere of openness in your group.

LISTENING FOR UNDERSTANDING—ACTIVE LISTENING

Once you have communicated both nonverbal and verbal signs of acceptance and have encouraged other people to talk, you can begin to listen for understanding. *The primary goal of listening for understanding is to discover how speakers think and feel.* What do they experience, desire, need, and want? How does the world look from their unique perspective? What does it mean to be them, in their world? This kind of listening—listening for understanding—is how therapists, psychologists, and psychiatrists are trained to listen to their clients. That's the way group members need to be heard by you at times. They need to be listened to for understanding.

The secret to listening for understanding is to test the accuracy of your message reception. The meaning of a message is not in the words of the message, but rather in the person sending the message and in the person receiving the message. In other words, meaning is in people, not in words. For example, the word *ball* can mean a football to me, a fun time to you, and a formal dance to someone else. The symbol or word *ball* was the same for all three of us, but the meanings we individually assigned to that word were very different.

Active listening is the process in which you restate in your own words what the speaker has said to clarify or confirm the accuracy of the message. Active listening most often involves the skill of **paraphrasing**, which is simply a restatement in your own words of the speaker's message.

Listening is often mistakenly viewed as a passive activity—the speaker talks and the listener listens. The speaker is active and verbal and the listener is passive and silent. When the speaker finishes talking, the assumption is that the message has been accurately received by the listener, with no observable effort or participation on the listener's part. What could be simpler? The speaker talks and the listener listens. But it's not so simple.

To ensure that the listener has accurately understood what the speaker has said, use the process of active listening. With active listening, the listener is an equal participant in the communication process. True communication requires the active participation of the listener as well as that of the speaker.

There are two types of active listening: active listening for **content** (accuracy) and active listening for **feelings** (empathy). The four basic steps to the active listening process are the same for both content and feelings. If you follow these four simple steps, you will master one of the fundamental skills in creating receptive communication as a listener.

Steps of Active Listening

Step 1.   The speaker makes a statement.

Step 2.   The listener paraphrases the speaker's statement ("Are you saying . . . ?").

Step 3.   The speaker rejects the paraphrase ("No, that's not what I meant.") or accepts the paraphrase ("Yes, that's what I meant.").

Step 4.   If rejected, the speaker clarifies the original statement (the process repeats). If accepted, the listener
is free to express a thought or feeling.

Don't overdo active listening. You don't want to sound like a parrot,
repeating every sentence the speaker says. This can be irritating to the
speaker and discourage communication as much as interrupting or
judging. Use active listening as you would spices in cooking—just
enough to clarify those statements you are unsure of.

Active Listening for Content

In a group, you will often use active listening for content to verify the
accuracy of what is being shared. Here are some examples of active listening for content:

Tim: These solutions we've proposed don't make it in my
opinion.

Sarah: *Are you saying* the solutions are not feasible?

Tim: That's exactly what I mean!

Thuy: I'm out of here if you guys don't include everyone in
the discussion.

Chip: *You mean* you're going to quit the group if everyone
isn't consulted?

Thuy: Yes. I feel very strongly about this.

Did you notice how, in both examples, Sarah and Chip actively
reflected what they thought they heard by asking, "Are you saying . . . ?"
and "You mean . . . ?" Remember not to parrot word for word what the
speaker has said. Just try to restate, in your own words, what the
speaker has said.

In the next dialogue, the first paraphrase is incorrect and the listener
and the speaker negotiate for shared meaning by using steps 3 and 4
of the active listening process:

Tammy: I think you should include Mark more in our group
discussions.

Hassan: *Are you saying* that I don't let Mark talk?

Tammy: No, you let him talk. But I would like you to recognize some of his comments.

Hassan: *You mean* acknowledge or compliment some of his proposals?

Tammy: Yes! It would make him feel more valued.

Hassan: I guess I don't acknowledge others enough. Sure, I'll try it.

Did you see how Tammy and Hassan had to repeat the process one more time to communicate the message accurately? This simple technique of actively reflecting the content of the message back to the speaker is effective in assuring the accurate reception of the thought or idea sent by the speaker.

There are three active listening techniques for testing the accuracy of the content sent by the speaker—the You technique, active listening questions, and active listening statements.

You technique. The most basic form of active listening is mirroring back to the speaker the content of the message with a question beginning with the word *you*. Here is an example of an active listening question:

Josh: I think I need to step back from my involvement in our group.

Maia: *You* think you need to take a break from chairing our group?

Josh: That's right. I'm getting a little burnt out.

Active listening questions. The second type of active listening involves asking the speaker if what you heard is correct by beginning your interpretation with questions such as "Do you mean . . . ?" "Are you saying . . . ?" "Do I understand you to say . . . ?" and "Are you feeling . . . ?" Here is an example of an active listening question:

Lena: Researching this problem is a blast.

Sue: *Are you saying* you're having fun interviewing the experts?

Lena: Yeah, I'm actually enjoying talking to the engineers.

Active listening statements. The final way you can reflect the content of the speaker's message is by using statements that introduce your interpretation. Here are some examples of phrases to use: "I hear you saying . . . ," "What you are saying . . . ," "What you are feeling is . . . ,"

"I understand you to mean . . . ," "It sounds like you . . . ," and "I'm feeling that you . . ." Here are a few examples of active listening statements:

> I hear you saying that you want a break from working Saturdays.
> It sounds like you wish you were in charge of the group.
> What you're saying is that you'd like to increase their stock options.

All three of these active listening techniques for content will help you more clearly understand the thoughts and ideas presented by others. They will enable you to make certain that the pictures you construct in your mind's eye match the ones others are attempting to communicate from their point of view. This same technique of active listening can also reflect our understanding of another person's feelings.

Active Listening for Feelings

Communicating in groups can often involve sharing feelings and discussing emotions. This is especially true if you're trying to help someone through a problem or difficulty. Rather than clarify and validate the accuracy of the speaker's message, the communication shifts levels to the speaker's feelings. To go beyond the content of what people are saying to the feelings they may also be attempting to communicate is a powerful way to encourage deeper connection and relationship.

> It is with the heart that one sees rightly; what is essential is invisible to the eye.
> ANTOINE DE SAINT-EXUPÉRY

Three ways you can listen for feelings in your communication with others are observing the speaker's nonverbal communication, reflecting the speaker's nonverbal behavior, and responding to the speaker's verbal communication.

Observing the speaker's nonverbal communication. Listen to the speaker's feelings not with your ears, but with your eyes. Feelings and emotions are communicated primarily at the nonverbal level, so during your next conversation, pay attention to facial expressions, posture, gestures, tone of voice, rate of speech, breathing, eye contact, touching behavior, and anything else you might observe. Be creative and listen for feelings with your ears and eyes!

Reflecting the speaker's nonverbal behavior. Often individuals are unaware of downcast eyes, a raised voice, an increased breathing rate, or a reddening face. Many times these nonverbal behaviors go unnoticed by speaker and listener. If you are observing any significant nonverbal behavior in another person, you may want to say so. Share your perception without attaching any value judgment to it. Rather than saying, "It looks like you're getting scared and frightened," say, "I notice that you keep looking out the window and your breathing is getting faster." This statement could invite the individual to talk about his or her feelings. Here are some phrases to use when listening to feelings:

I notice that you're arriving later and later to our meetings.
I see that you're looking at the clock.
I hear you sigh when I . . .
I notice that you're smiling when I talk about . . .

Responding to the speaker's verbal communication. A speaker may verbally invite you to communicate at the feeling level of communication by sharing a feeling statement with you, such as "I'm feeling happy," "I'm feeling upset," or "This situation makes me feel discouraged." Be sensitive to such feeling statements and respond to them with a paraphrase to encourage the speaker to explore or comment further. Here are some examples:

I'm feeling a little tense.
So, you're feeling uptight?

This situation encourages me.
Sounds like you're feeling optimistic.

The purpose of paraphrasing or reflecting the feeling statement is to prove that you have received the message and to encourage the speaker to remain at the feeling level by exploring or expanding upon his or her feeling statement.

A second way you can listen for feelings is to respond to the speaker's specific invitations to communicate at the feeling level. When the speaker asks you how you're feeling about a particular issue, person, or situation, respond with an appropriate feeling response instead of remaining at the content level. Here are some examples:

Are you happy with the group's decision?
Yes, I'm pleased we decided to donate the money.

Am I making you feel comfortable?
Yes, I'm not feeling nervous or frightened.

You can also issue an invitation yourself. Follow up a speaker's content statement with a feeling-level question. This is one of the basic tools of therapists and counselors, especially when clients are unaware of or unwilling to explore their feelings. Here are some examples of feeling-level questions:

I might be promoted to manager. (content level)
How are you feeling about that? (feeling-level question)

I'm discovering that the job is requiring more time than I
   thought. (content level)
Are you feeling overburdened? (feeling-level question)

By responding to the speaker's content statement with a feeling-level question, you encourage the speaker to share at a deeper level. There are times during group discussion when the sharing of feelings is beneficial, especially when emotions are running high during disagreement or conflict. By inviting speakers to share their feelings, you encourage a deeper level of interaction and understanding.

ADVANTAGES OF ACTIVE LISTENING

Active listening has a number of advantages. First, and most obvious, it proves understanding. It assures both speaker and listener that the message sent was indeed the message received. That is what is meant by listening for understanding.

Second, active listening involves the listener. No longer does the listener passively sit and assume he has received the message accurately. The listener must participate in the process of communication and become involved in the message negotiation.

Third, active listening relieves the listener from having to act as judge, teacher, or rescuer. The listener simply reflects the message back to the speaker, but doesn't problem-solve, judge, give advice, or perform a hundred other intrusive activities listeners are often inclined to do.

Fourth, the speaker has a safe place to disclose thoughts and feelings without being threatened, criticized, or punished. The speaker can share, explore, and consider her thoughts and feelings without fear of evaluation.

Fifth, active listening develops trust between the speaker and the listener. It isn't very often an individual is given the opportunity to share what is really on his mind or deep in her heart without being attacked, rejected, or rescued. This is the most important reward of listening for understanding. The speaker trusts you.

GUIDELINES FOR ACTIVE LISTENING

Your skill in reflecting the content and feelings of other group members will greatly enhance the accuracy of the group's communication and will serve to create a more open and productive group atmosphere. As you use your active listening skills, keep the following guidelines in mind.

Avoid Parroting

A common mistake the beginning active listener makes is to paraphrase, word for word, the speaker's statement. Just like a parrot, the listener will repeat almost verbatim the words of the speaker. Here are a couple of examples of parroting:

> Hector: I feel happy.
> Sam: You feel happy?
>
> Sally: I'm having second thoughts about leaving.
> Nadya: You're having second thoughts about leaving?

The main disadvantage to parroting is that the listener doesn't prove true understanding of the speaker's statement. The listener merely repeats the exact wording of the statement and does not process the statement into his or her own words. A second disadvantage to parroting is the "echo" effect, which quickly becomes tiring to hear. Be creative! Put the speaker's statement into your own words.

Avoid Overuse of Active Listening

Nothing is more irritating than using active listening to mirror every statement you hear during a conversation. This can drive people crazy. You should reserve active listening for those occasions when:

1. You need to clarify the speaker's message.
2. The speaker needs to feel understood by you.
3. The speaker needs to vent or process feelings.
4. You and the speaker are in conflict.

If you use active listening about once every five statements you hear during a conversation, you will not only improve the quality of the communication, but you will also dramatically improve the quality of your relationships in small groups.

Avoid Inappropriate Active Listening

Sometimes active listening is inappropriate. Although there are no fast and easy rules on inappropriate active listening, you'll soon get a gut feeling for it after a while. Here are some obvious examples:

Ann: What time is it, Omar?
Omar: Are you asking what time it is?

Nancy: The house is burning!
Ted: You're saying the house is burning?

In both examples, Omar and Ted inappropriately used active listening. Ann's question and Nancy's statement did not require clarification from the listeners. If these were real conversations, few people would blame the speakers for kicking the listeners in the shins!

This chapter examined the skill of active listening—a method of listening for understanding—so you can make others feel understood when they speak to you. Your ability to listen for understanding in a group will not only ensure that you have understood what others are saying, but also demonstrate an openness and desire to encourage others to express themselves without judgment or evaluation. This might be one of the most important ingredients in creating effective groups.

4.1 Listening the Wrong Way

The next time you're talking with a friend, try listening the wrong way—with a nonunderstanding listening style. Don't tell your friend what you are doing. Listen for your ego. Judge everything your friend says in terms of whether you agree with him or her. Try not to be too obvious or obnoxious, but in a gentle way verbally judge the content of what your friend says during the conversation. See if you can listen the "wrong way" for a minute or two.

Did your friend notice your listening response style? What did your friend say or do to indicate that he or she noticed your change in listening (at least, I hope this isn't your usual style of listening)? How did listening the wrong way affect or modify the content of the discussion? How did listening the wrong way affect or modify the way your friend communicated? How did it feel to you? Did it feel familiar? Did it feel strange? Who listens to you in this style? How does it feel to you to be judged when you share with another? Did the two of you discuss this little experiment after you shared the intent of this experiment? What did you discover about yourself?

4.2 Listening for Understanding

With a different friend, try listening for understanding (active listening) for four or five minutes. Don't tell your friend about your little experiment. Simply slip into an active listening style of communicating without verbally noting the change. Carry on your part of the conversation. If your friend asks you a question, reply. The purpose of the experiment is for you to listen in a way that provides you with a greater understanding of what your friend thinks and feels. Use questions or statements that begin with "You're saying . . . ," "You're feeling . . . ," "What I hear you saying is . . . ," "You feel that . . . ?" "Sounds like you . . . ," and so on. Use some variety in your listening for understanding. Don't reflect every statement your friend makes. Try active listening once or twice every minute—that's enough. The rest of the time, keep up your end of the conversation. After the conversation is over, share with your friend that you were experimenting with a new way of listening—a method that would improve your understanding.

Did your friend notice your listening response style? What did your friend say or do that indicated he or she noticed your change in listening? How did listening for understanding affect or modify the content of the discussion? How did listening for understanding affect or modify the way your friend communicated with you? How did it feel to you? What did you discover about yourself as you attempted to listen for understanding?

4.3 Group Paraphrasing

In your group, have members make a statement about how they perceive a specific weakness in the group's performance (either task or social dimension). Then have the person immediately to the right of each speaker attempt to paraphrase (listening for understanding) the content of the statement to the speaker's satisfaction. If the paraphrase is correct, the speaker says, "That's exactly what I mean!" and the listener makes his or her own statement about a group weakness. If the paraphrase is incorrect, the listener tries a second time. If the second paraphrase is incorrect, then any group member can offer a paraphrase of the speaker's original statement.

How did the exercise work? What made some group members more successful at paraphrasing than others? How did it feel to paraphrase others? How did it feel to be paraphrased by others? How might you use listening for understanding in your group work or personal life?

CHAPTER FIVE

Problem Solving in Groups

Every problem provides an opportunity
for you to do your best.

DUKE ELLINGTON

t was two hours into a meeting that seemed to drag on forever. I sat in one corner of the room observing seven men and women, all assembly-line production team managers at a local computer company, discussing the problem of employee language barriers. Some managers had to cope with six different languages in their production crews of thirty people. I was one of a three-member communication consulting team hired to observe three two-hour meetings and then suggest specific ways this group could improve its communication behavior.

After three meetings, the managers had yet to agree on a solution to the problem. Our observation team met later to compare notes and view segments of the videotaped discussions. We made five interesting observations about the group's problem-solving behavior.

The group spent only twenty minutes of the six-hour discussion time analyzing the scope and nature of the problem. They took two and a half hours explaining, clarifying, and defending their own proposals. The group generated only five solutions during the three meetings. More than eighty minutes of the discussion time was spent sharing tangential complaints, company gossip, and other topics not directly related to the topic. Finally, the group made only six attempts to provide any structure to the discussion in the form of summaries or reviews.

The production managers were surprised by our observations and most astonished by the self-centered nature of each individual's behavior and the group's inability to keep the discussion focused.

In the workshops we presented, our team trained the managers in problem analysis, active listening, brainstorming techniques, and discussion-guiding behaviors. The problem-solving sessions after the training were much more focused, creative, and productive. The eventual solutions to the language barrier problems were far different and more effective than the ones originally proposed. What was most heartening to us were their increased skills and confidence in working as a team.

This chapter will provide you with a systematic approach to solving problems in a small group. Like life, however, there are many roads that lead to a satisfying and worthwhile experience. The problem-solving agenda we will explore is one of many approaches, but it is the one followed most often in the United States to find workable solutions to problems challenging small groups. As you work in problem-solving groups, strive to remain as open, flexible, and creative as you can while addressing the problems you have to solve.

MYTHS OF SMALL-GROUP PROBLEM SOLVING

The assumptions we bring into the small-group problem-solving process directly and powerfully influence the manner in which we participate and feel about working with others in groups. The following are some false assumptions about the small-group process.

Myth 1: Only One Solution Exists to a Problem

When a group gets together to solve a problem, there is a tendency for the group to think there can be only one "right" answer to the problem. Maybe this is a carryover from our school days, when each question on a quiz or examination had only one "correct answer." When working in a problem-solving group, don't limit yourself by looking for only one solution to a problem—look for as many as you can. Challenge all group members who feel they have discovered the "right" answer. Always work to broaden and increase the possibilities and solutions. Think big! Think of the many!

Myth 2: Our Solution Is the Best Solution

Once the group has weathered the storms of the problem-solving process, there is often a feeling or attitude of invincibility or infallibility. Taken to an extreme, this phenomenon is known as groupthink— the group attitude that it can do no wrong (discussed in Chapter 9). Be aware that the assumption that the group's decision or solution is the best, simply because the group invested effort in its creation, can be false.

The group needs to challenge the myth of "our solution is the best." It would be better if group members adopted a tentative attitude or approach to their solution by saying, "This is the best solution we can come up with at the moment. But we are staying open to the possibility of discovering other solutions, maybe even better solutions, in the days to come." An attitude of openness and discovery, rather than of arrogance and closed-mindedness, will keep the group healthy, wealthy (in the spiritual sense), and wise.

> Nothing is more dangerous than an idea, when it's the only one we have.
> ÉMILE CHARTIER

Myth 3: Two Heads Are Always Better Than One

Getting together with other people to solve problems is based on the notion that "two heads are better than one," and that a group of people can provide more information, experience, and creativity than a single person can. But for this to occur, members must possess some level of mutual respect, cooperation, and skill. They must also be willing to come together and join forces so that they can build upon their pool of information, experiences, and resources in a spirit of cooperation.

If willingness, mutual respect, cooperation, and goodwill are not present, then the consequences can be harmful, counterproductive, and even disastrous. Working in groups is no picnic, as you are well aware. It exacts a price from each group member in time and effort. But the benefits can outweigh the costs.

Myth 4: No Conflict Will Arise

Another assumption many people bring to group work is that there should be no conflict during the process of problem solving. Aren't we grown, mature adults? Aren't we rational, logical people? Well, we are and we aren't. I am beginning to think I'm not as rational, logical, and mature as I once thought when I was younger, especially when I'm working under pressure or during extreme stress. The more honest I am with myself, the more willing I am to admit to my occasional self-centeredness, my unwillingness to listen, and my reluctance to compromise.

Groups may experience greater conflict after members feel a certain level of security and trust within the group. This is natural. Whenever people share ideas, conflict will arise. This isn't bad; it just comes with the territory. Without conflict, group members cannot create the solutions their problems require. Like labor pains during childbirth, there is no creation without some suffering. The group must experience conflict to be successful.

Myth 5: I Must Like and Be Liked by Everyone

A tremendous amount of emotional energy is spent on the belief that you should like each group member and that each member should like you. When interpersonal conflict arises within a group, remember the One-Third Rule. My theory is that in any group of people, one-third of them will like you no matter what you do, one-third will not like you no matter what you do, and one-third don't care about you no matter what you do. It would be nice if everyone liked everyone else in the group, but unfortunately, such a mutual admiration society doesn't happen often. So don't lose sleep over someone's sneer, snide remark, or personal attack. It comes with the territory. Keep in mind the One-Third Rule and you'll be easier on yourself and on others. You don't have to be liked or approved of by everyone.

Myth 6: Everything Must Go My Way

There is a subtle, almost unconscious assumption that if things don't go the way you want them to go, you should be disappointed, upset, or even angry. One of the important lessons in life is that you don't always get what you want. In fact, you would most likely be in a terrible mess if every one of your wishes, fantasies, and dreams came true. Can you even begin to imagine the hideous life you would have right now if even half of the wishes you dreamed about during your high-school years came true?

An important discovery I make about myself each time I work with a problem-solving group is that my ideas aren't always the best, my suggestions aren't always the most insightful, and my intuitions are often proven wrong. What I find refreshing in working with a group is a renewed sense of humility, practice in letting go of what I think is right and good, and a deeper appreciation for the beauty and creativity of others. I discover I am moved by other human beings in ways that are unexpected and sometimes even profound.

Myth 7: Every Problem Has a Solution

Many people believe that if there is a problem, there has to be a workable, acceptable solution floating around somewhere in the universe. But this may not always be the case. Today, some experts have somberly pronounced that there might be no current solutions to such significant problems as the destruction of the ozone layer, the continued pollution of our oceans, and the rise in violent crime. I don't know whether this is true, but the possibility remains that there may be no solutions to these particular problems based on our current technology and resources. Likewise, your group may encounter a problem that cannot be solved with the resources, technology, and manpower available.

Psychiatrist Carl Jung had an interesting thought about the nature of problems. He felt that many problems in life may have no solution. "They might never be solved," he cautioned, "but merely outgrown." Maybe some problems cannot be solved; we merely outgrow or lose interest in them.

If you keep challenging these seven myths about small-group problem solving, you will be a wiser, more effective group participant. Now that you have the right attitude toward working with others in groups, we can introduce some decision-making techniques.

DECISION-MAKING TECHNIQUES

Each of us makes hundreds of decisions every day. Most of these decisions are relatively insignificant—what shoes to wear, where to go to lunch, and when to go to sleep. Other decisions are more significant: Should I leave this job? Can I afford this home? Should I end this relationship?

When it comes to these more significant life questions, how do you make your decisions? Some people consult horoscopes; others flip a coin. One person will ask the advice of a parent; another person will pray for a sign. Some go to a mountaintop and meditate until a direction becomes clear. But when it comes to small-group decision making, we do not always have the luxury to consult these more intimate, idiosyncratic methods of making decisions. The small-group decision-making process is less private, more public, and relies on five more widely used decision-making techniques.

Decision by the Leader

Decision by the leader calls for the leader to decide for the group, either after discussion with the group or without the group's contributions. Traditionally, many American business corporations have made their decisions in this fashion. The advantages of this method of decision making are that it minimizes wasted time, reinforces the traditional hierarchical business structure, and can be efficient in making administrative decisions. The disadvantages can be a lack of commitment to the solution by the group, superficial or minimal group discussion and analysis, and the development of an adversarial relationship between leader and group members.

A variation of this method includes decision by a designated authority or expert to whom the group defers decision-making authority because the authority possesses more expertise and experience than the group has. Another method is decision by an executive committee or subgroup made up of group members. This method works well if the group is overloaded with work and total group participation is not feasible.

Decision by Majority Rule

The most widely used method of group decision making is majority rule or voting. We've all experienced the desperate plea for conflict resolution when someone yells, "Let's vote on it! I'm tired of arguing about this topic!" The vote is taken and the matter is settled. Or is it really?

The disadvantages of majority rule are that there are always winners and losers and that majority rule provides no protection for the minority. Additionally, the losers often suffer because they feel their position was discarded by the majority. Many times, the minority will work to sabotage the implementation of the solution or decision. So, the majority should never ignore the minority simply because they lost.

The advantages are that decisions can be made quickly and time can be saved. Majority rule is effective for procedural matters, such as voting on meeting times, placement of items on the agenda, and other administrative issues. But decision making that needs commitment from the entire group requires a different way of deciding.

Decision by Compromise

The compromise method of decision making is a bartering technique: "If you give us this, then we'll give you that." Members of one point of view will give up some aspect of their solution in exchange for support from other group members. Compromise combines aspects of the most popular solutions being discussed.

In theory, compromise doesn't sound all that bad. Isn't life compromise? But in reality, compromise often results in low commitment to the solution, because the solution can be so weakened or diluted as to make it ineffective or unacceptable.

Compromise is good when the viewpoint of some members is incompatible with the viewpoint of other members. Compromise permits the discussion to continue, whereas lack of compromise would have killed discussion long ago.

The disadvantage to compromise is that it is often used too early in discussion and prevents productive exploration of alternatives. It also produces decisions or solutions that are watered-down, "averaging out" differences between various points of view.

Decision by Arbitration

Sometimes decision making needs to come from outside the group or groups in conflict. For instance, a dispute between labor and management often requires settlement by a third party—an arbitrator. The **arbitrator** is an impartial third party, whose decision both sides have agreed to be binding. In other words, both groups will accept the arbitrator's decision.

The advantage of this decision-making method is that the arbitrator will break an impasse or stalemate. Arbitration gets the ball rolling again, whereas an impasse between the two sides could polarize them even more, increase tension and hostility between the sides, and prevent compromise from ever occurring. The disadvantage is similar to that of majority rule. The loser in the decision must accept the ruling of the arbitrator and in doing so must also accept the fate of the minority.

Decision by Consensus

A highly effective decision-making method for a small group is consensus. **Consensus** requires that all group members find the decision acceptable. The decision may *not* be each member's first choice, but each member regards the decision as acceptable and workable.

Consensus is different from compromise in that the final decision is not an "averaged-out," hybrid choice between two different points of view. The decision is a new, third point of view that each group member regards as workable and acceptable.

A test for consensus during group discussion is the question "Can you live with it for a period of time?" not "Is this your number-one choice?" or "Are you happy with this decision?" or "Is this the perfect solution?" The question "Can you live with it for a period of time?" helps the group determine whether the decision is (1) workable and (2) acceptable.

An advantage of decision by consensus is that it increases member satisfaction with the decision, because *all* group members must buy into the decision of the group and *any* member can prevent or block the acceptance of a decision. So the ultimate decision is the product of thorough discussion, which also can promote a stronger social dimension in the group and increasing commitment to the implementation of the solution.

A disadvantage of decision making by consensus is that it requires a tremendous amount of time. Whereas the other four methods of decision making—by leader, majority rule, compromise, and arbitration—can terminate discussion with the imposition of the decision, consensus demands that members talk until they discover a decision that is workable and acceptable to all.

Here are five guidelines for reaching consensus within a group:

1. **Listen to everyone's position.** Present your views and positions. Then *listen* to the views and positions of the other group members. Don't argue for your own position.
2. **Look for acceptable options.** Don't assume this is a contest. Try not to view the discussion as an activity that someone has to win and someone has to lose. Look for the next acceptable option for all members.
3. **Accept conflict.** Difference of opinion is natural. Critically listen to and evaluate the arguments and evidence of others. Yield only to the views and opinions that make sense to you. Differences of opinion make for higher-quality decisions. Don't avoid conflict.
4. **Don't use conflict-reducing techniques.** Don't vote, flip coins, compromise, or average. These techniques require someone to win and someone to lose.
5. **Include the participation of all members.** Make certain all group members are included in the decision-making process. Ask low-verbal members for their opinions, reactions, and feelings.

Follow these guidelines to help your group find an acceptable and workable solution.

DISCUSSION QUESTIONS

One of the most important tools in small-group decision making and problem solving is the discussion question. The discussion question helps in problem identification. Problems need to be formulated into a discussion question to help focus the group's thinking, research, and discussion. As you will see, different types of discussion questions reveal and produce entirely different kinds of decisions and solutions to a problem. The three types of discussion questions are questions of fact, value, and policy.

Questions of Fact

A **question of fact** asks if something is true, if something is occurring, or if something has already occurred. Questions of fact involve who, what, when, where, and why questions. Examples of questions of fact are:

> How much money do our competitors spend on advertising?
> When did production begin to increase more than 10 percent annually?
> Who served as group leader during our last meeting?

Questions of Value

A **question of value** asks for a judgment on whether something is good or bad, right or wrong. Such questions involve an individual's subjective opinion regarding matters of taste. These questions are more difficult for a group to agree on, because the values, tastes, and beliefs of each member can be so different. Examples of value questions are:

> Is it good public relations to donate our product to charitable causes?
> Is our new design pleasing to the eye?
> Who was the best group leader during the last quarter?

Questions of Policy

A **question of policy** asks for discussion on which course of action should be taken. Questions of policy are generally the result of a problem or situation needing change or improvement. To answer a question of policy, the group must also answer many questions of fact and value in their problem-solving deliberations. Examples of questions of policy are:

> What should our policy be toward increased competition in advertising?
> What should we do if we increase profits by more than 30 percent annually?
> What should our policy be if group leaders don't meet minimal standards?

Questions of policy are the beginning focal point of a group's attempts to solve a problem. The question of policy should be as specific as possible. Vague and general terms must be avoided. Limit your question of policy to only one issue at a time. Multiple-issue policy questions tend to scatter your group's research, energy, and focus. "What should be our hospital's policy toward rising surgical costs, malpractice litigation regarding psychiatric care, and custodial demands for pay raises?" is a question of policy that covers too many issues. A more specific question would be "What should our hospital's policy be toward rising surgical costs?"

THE STANDARD PROBLEM-SOLVING AGENDA

The most common response to problems in corporations and organizations is to blame or defend. If there is a problem, many people will immediately look for someone to blame or will defend themselves from the blame of others. So, when groups are formed to solve a problem, whether in a business, a school, or a neighborhood, the initial response of group members is often to blame or defend. A more productive approach to solving problems is to follow the standard problem-solving agenda.

Most current problem-solving agendas are based upon John Dewey's reflective thinking model, whether they include all the steps he provided in *How We Think* or some modification of them.

The problem-solving agenda presented here is a modified version of Dewey's model, with the addition of an orientation step at the beginning.

PROBLEM-SOLVING AGENDA

Step 1. Check in.
Step 2. Analyze the problem.
Step 3. Brainstorm solutions.
Step 4. Evaluate the better solutions.
Step 5. Reach consensus on the best solution.
Step 6. Implement the solution.

The variations in the quality of decisions arrived at by groups can be accounted for by the ability of group members to perform four important decision-making functions. They are the effective assessment and discussion of (1) the problem, (2) the criteria for the solution, (3) the strengths of the proposed solutions, and (4) the weaknesses of the proposed solutions (Hirokawa, 1988). You will notice that these four functions are incorporated into the standard agenda we will examine in detail.

Step I: Check In

The first step the group must take is to provide members with the opportunity to establish a supportive and trusting social dimension. Without a healthy social dimension, the group will not be able to function to maximum effectiveness.

Initially, the check-in period may require a substantial amount of time—perhaps even the entire meeting. The check-in encourages group members to introduce themselves and disclose any pertinent professional and personal information they feel may be helpful.

After the group has established a supportive, friendly social dimension, the check-in step of each meeting becomes less involved. Usually, members will take thirty to sixty seconds to tell how things have been going in their lives since the group last met. Much useful information can be provided during the group's check-in, and I've found these five minutes to be important to maintaining the group's social dimension.

Step 2: Analyze the Problem

Analysis of the problem is the second step the group takes to solve a problem. Fruitful discussion at this stage requires that group members research the problem before coming to the meeting so that they are ready to discuss the following questions:

1. What is the problem?
2. What is the question of policy?
3. What is the nature of the problem?
4. Whom does the problem affect?
5. How serious is the problem?
6. What are causes of the problem?
7. What solutions have been attempted before?
8. What will happen if the problem is not solved?
9. What are the constraints for a workable solution?
10. What are five possible solutions that satisfy your criteria?

These ten questions for problem analysis are the most frequently asked questions of problem-solving groups. *Feel free to modify, delete, and add to this list as you and your group see fit.* The next chapter discusses how to research these questions. But for now, be aware that the quality of your group's research will determine the quality of information for the remainder of the group's activities.

Step 3: Brainstorm Solutions

The primary purpose of the brainstorming step is to generate a large number of ideas without evaluating them. The most serious threat to a workable and acceptable solution to any problem is the group's inability to generate more than two or three solutions.

I believe a group should never stop brainstorming until it has generated at least thirty possible solutions—not two or three, but thirty!

During the brainstorming process, group members sit in a circle and contribute possible solutions to the problem under study. Members write down and number every suggestion made (including their own). The primary rule is that members cannot evaluate any idea. There is no rationale, explanation, or justification for each suggestion, simply the suggestion. The brainstorming session continues until the group reaches at least thirty suggestions.

> We all know your idea is crazy.
> The question is,
> whether it's crazy enough.
> NEILS BOHR

Here are some guidelines for a successful brainstorming session:

1. Devote a specific amount of time to brainstorming.
2. Every member must take notes, numbering each item.
3. Evaluation of any idea is not permitted.

4. Questions, storytelling, explanations, and tangential talking are not permitted.
5. Quantity of ideas, not quality, is desired.
6. The wilder the ideas the better.
7. Combine ideas.

You will discover some group members enjoy this process of generating ideas without evaluation. We're accustomed to it in our daily lives.

A variation of this brainstorming technique is called the **Nominal Group Technique (NGT)**. Group members individually generate a list of solutions to a problem, and then get together to record their lists on a blackboard for the entire group to consider. The advantages and disadvantages of each solution are not discussed, although clarification is permitted. Each group member then selects his or her five most favorite ideas and ranks their order on a card. Cards are collected, the rankings are averaged, and the solution with the highest average is the winner. The NGT is helpful, especially if the group is limited by time constraints, but its primary weakness is the lack of analysis of the solutions proposed. The group must invest time and effort in the discussion of the best possible solutions.

Step 4: Evaluate the Better Solutions

Now's the time to slip back into a more critical-thinking frame of mind. Before your group evaluates the better solutions against the criteria you have established in step 2, you need to spend some time throwing out the ridiculous, illegal, and impractical suggestions created during the brainstorming session. This is when the numbers come in handy. Instead of reading the entire proposal or idea to discard or throw out, you simply announce the number. If members agree, they'll tell you. If not, they'll tell you. Either way, using the number instead of reading off the entire suggestion or idea each time will save you time, energy, and effort.

Once the group has ten to fifteen ideas or solutions worth examining, then the real task of step 4 begins—discussion of the strengths and weaknesses of the better solutions on the list. Here are some guidelines for a more effective discussion:

1. Discuss one solution at a time.
2. Consider both its strengths and its weaknesses.

3. Consider how many constraints each solution satisfies.
4. Move to another solution quickly. Don't get stuck.
5. Avoid lumping solutions into one large conglomeration.
6. Don't be afraid to challenge a solution. Now is the time to share your reservations.

Evaluation of the better solutions will take time. Keep these guidelines in mind when considering the better solutions. Speak your mind. Now is the time to voice your reservations as well as your preferences. Above all, listen for understanding while other members are sharing their reservations and preferences.

Step 5: Reach Consensus on the Best Solution

As the group discusses the better solutions, two or possibly three solutions will keep surfacing during the discussion. When you notice this occurring, mention it to the group. Let members know the group may be arriving at some agreement or common ground.

A second minibrainstorming session may be appropriate at this time to generate a few related solutions to the two or three remaining in hopes of discovering one solution that is workable and acceptable to all group members. Remember, for consensus to occur, everyone must find the solution workable and acceptable.

To test for consensus, ask group members if they can live with a particular solution. They might object, stating it's not their first choice or they're not overly pleased with the solution. Just smile and repeat the question that tests for consensus: "But can you live with this solution for a period of time?"

After the group has reached consensus on a solution, take a break and celebrate. Remember the reinforcement phase of group development? Call out for pizza and soft drinks. The group deserves it!

Step 6: Implement the Solution

After you've cleaned up the pizza crumbs and empty cans, the group needs to implement the solution, which involves three steps—planning a timetable, assigning implementation tasks, and evaluating the implementation process. If the group is not required to implement the solution, this final step can be disregarded.

Plan a timetable. The group needs to divide the implementation of the solution into its component objectives and assign dates for the completion of those objectives. Be as specific as possible when you describe the component objectives.

Assign tasks. Assign individual members to complete the various tasks. Make certain each member knows the task and the date by which the task must be accomplished. Everyone should have the phone numbers or e-mail addresses of all group members, because communication is critical to the success of the project at this stage.

Evaluate implementation. Evaluation of the group's effectiveness in implementing the solution to the problem can be accomplished during a face-to-face meeting or conference call. Changes in procedure or approach may need to be made for future groups. Additional resources may need to be secured. Individual members may need to be encouraged, pushed, or congratulated. If the implementation was a success and all members are satisfied with their performance and that of the group, once again, I suggest a social get-together to celebrate a job well done.

Reanalyze the problem (if necessary). If the solution fails to meet the group's expectations or standards, members may need to return to the beginning of the standard agenda and reanalyze the problem in step 2. Evaluation of the implementation may have provided valuable information or a new perspective that was not initially available to the group. Many times, it is only after a solution is implemented that incomplete, inaccurate, or faulty analysis of the problem becomes apparent. In any case, the group can return to step 2 and begin the entire process again.

THE CIRCULAR NATURE OF PROBLEM SOLVING

The standard agenda provides groups with the most complete and time-tested problem-solving method (Wood et al., 1986), but that does not mean groups necessarily follow a linear, step-by-step process when they solve problems in the real world. That's why I suggest that groups *reanalyze the problem* in step 6. It enables a group to return full circle to the beginning of the agenda and begin the process again with additional information and new insight.

This circular approach to problem solving is supported by the research of Marshall Poole (1981), who discovered that 23 percent of the decisions in problem-solving groups resulted from a strictly linear, decision-making sequence of phases, while approximately 47 percent of the decisions were made in repeated cycles of focusing on the problem, then the solution, then back to the problem. Finally, 30 percent of the decisions were made by the groups focusing their discussion only on solutions with little or no attention given to the analysis of the problem.

These findings are helpful when you use the standard agenda because they serve as a reminder that group problem solving is not always a linear, step-by-step process, but is more often circular and dynamic, not following clear-cut divisions. Your group may begin with the analysis of the problem, then skip to a discussion of a solution, and return to problem analysis. Or, as mentioned earlier, group members may actually implement a solution, only to discover that they need to return to the beginning of the agenda and begin again with additional information and insight. Don't get upset when these things occur—that's simply the circular nature of problem solving.

> Arriving at one goal is the starting point of another.
> J O H N D E W E Y

Don't take this, however, as license to disregard the standard agenda and engage in a nonstructured approach to solving problems. Research repeatedly reminds us that a systematic approach to solving problems will help increase a group's effectiveness in the analysis of the problem, generation of possible solutions, and decision quality (Hirokawa, 1985; Gouran, 1991). Your goal is to give the group the flexibility to engage in a dynamic, circular decision-making process, within a systematic approach to solving problems.

The standard agenda will provide you and your group with a time-tested systematic approach to problem solving. The group's flexibility in its application ensures that group members will be given the freedom to do their best work.

BEING MORE CREATIVE

Even though you can approach any problem using the standard problem-solving agenda, your group's success will be determined to a large extent by the creativity each member brings to the process. The problem-solving process will not work if the group doesn't generate creative solutions to the problems. All the researched information, skillfully guided discussion, and eloquently expressed opinions will ultimately fall flat if group members lack the creativity to produce solutions and adapt to the changing demands of the group process. Here are some specific things you can do to increase your creativity in your group.

Going for the second right answer. One of the most helpful habits you can get into for increasing your creativity is to think in terms of multiple solutions to questions or problems. Our educational experiences from kindergarten to college usually focus on the students finding the one "right" answer to the question posed by the teacher. After years of trying to find the "right" answer, we are generally satisfied when our group proposes an answer to a question or a solution to a problem and we stop the process at that moment. To encourage creativity, go for the second "right" answer, and the third, and the fourth, and the fifth "right" answer. The brainstorming process in the problem-solving agenda requires us to generate many possible solutions to a problem, but you need to extend that mindset of looking for many answers to questions and multiple solutions to problems during all the phases of problem solving. Go for the second right answer.

Seeing it from a different angle. Another helpful habit that encourages creativity is seeing events, people, and things from a different perspective. We normally hold one predominant perception, interpretation, idea, or belief about most things in our lives. When working with others in groups, it's best if you can be open and flexible as you listen to the thoughts and opinions of others. Put some effort into seeing the world through the eyes of others. More important, offer different interpretations to events, people, and things that may not usually be held by the group.

One simple technique that encourages different perceptions is the reframing technique, which begins with the phrase "Another way of looking at it is . . ." Suppose the group feels that a certain solution is not feasible. You can use the reframing technique to help the group see the same solution from a slightly different angle. For instance, your group feels that holding an off-site training seminar at a college campus isn't feasible—it's too much hassle to get there, the classrooms are old-fashioned, and it could evoke bad memories for some workers. Instead of agreeing with this perception, you could reframe the same proposal by saying, "Another way of looking at this is one day in a college classroom may be just what our group needs to stimulate some of the youthful perspective, optimism, and fun we had during our college days."

By seeing something from a slightly different angle, reframing can open up an entirely new way for the group to view an idea, option, or solution. Be a source of creativity by looking at things from different perspectives.

Breaking the rules. A third habit you can acquire to increase your creativity is to occasionally break rules—nothing illegal, irresponsible, or impolite. But often, creativity can be unleashed when you venture beyond the boundaries of the rules or norms that dictate group behavior. Instead of always following the standard problem-solving agenda, bend the rules and change the order of the agenda. Start from the last step and work backward to the first step. Instead of always meeting in the conference room, suggest that the group meet at a pizzeria or park. Begin the meeting with a compliment session, take twice as many breaks during the meeting for snacks, or maybe limit every member to only five comments per hour to allow low-verbal members to participate more. Whatever you do, try modifying the rules once in a while to break out of the usual mold of predictable behavior and venture into the unknown. You just may stumble onto something very new, exciting, and worthwhile.

Listening to famous voices. A fun way to increase your creativity and stretch your imagination is to pose your group's question or problem to a famous person, either living or dead. How would Moses, Jesus, Mohammed, Eleanor Roosevelt, Abraham Lincoln, Harriet Tubman, Helen Keller, Albert Einstein, Arnold Schwarzenegger, Martha Stewart, Bill Gates, Katie Couric, Leonardo da Vinci, Jane Austen, William Shakespeare, Mother Teresa, or Michael Jordan answer the question or solve the problem your group is considering? By seeing the question or problem from the perspective of these and other famous individuals, you could be opening yourself up to an entirely new and fresh perspective or understanding of your problem. Group members can even role-play these famous thinkers and discuss the group's ideas from a very different frame of reference. Try imagining the advice and counsel of different people you admire and respect, and see where it takes you. It just may be what the group needs to get started in a new direction.

Having fun for a change. One final suggestion for increasing your creativity is to have fun. Normally, problem-solving groups are faced with serious issues that require immediate attention. The content and tone of the discussion is often serious, analytical, and urgent. When group members take on this demeanor, their thinking can become rigid and unimaginative. Thus, the creativity of the group is thwarted by the ever-increasing seriousness of the group's interactions.

When you're sensing that the group is getting stuck in a serious, inflexible posture, which discourages or eliminates creative thinking, you can try having fun by doing some rather outrageous things. Suggest that the problem really isn't a problem, but that it actually prevents worse problems from happening. Agree that the problem is really a problem, but that nothing should be done about it yet because the problem may just solve itself. Reverse the assumptions for the group.

For example, if the group is assuming that solutions that are within the budget are desirable, reverse this assumption by suggesting that solutions that exceed the budget are superior because they will force the department to go broke and then upper management will finally become involved in the problem-solving process. Find something about the problem to joke about, or joke about the group itself. Sometimes humor and a good laugh can have a healthy effect upon the group.

The successful group must be creative and flexible to succeed. Your willingness and ability to bring some creativity to the group will contribute to the ultimate success of the group's work. Be open to ways that can encourage and develop your creativity as you participate in groups that work.

How you approach the problems that will face you in life will determine, to a great extent, the quality of your life. Will you deny problems, rush to the first solution that comes to mind, or systematically approach them with knowledge, creativity, and thoughtful consideration? In this chapter, you have been given a systematic approach to solving problems—the standard problem-solving agenda. As you work in groups, remember to slow down and devote the time and energy to really understand the problem, to generate a list of many possible solutions, and to allow thorough discussion as the group decides on the best solution. You will discover the best solutions by creating the right circumstances, both in your group work and with yourself.

INDIVIDUAL AND GROUP EXERCISES

5.1 Analyzing a Personal Problem

The beauty of the standard problem-solving agenda is its applicability to your personal life as well as to groups. Examine a problem or conflict you are currently experiencing (or have experienced) in your personal life. It doesn't matter whether it's a relationship problem, an employment issue, or a living situation. After you've identified a specific problem from your personal life, complete the following questions:

1. What specifically is the problem? (Describe in one sentence.)
2. Whom does the problem affect?
3. How serious is the problem? Circle the appropriate conditions:
   I think about it occasionally. It affects my relationships with others.
   I think about it often. It affects my job/school performance.
   I obsess about the problem. It affects my daily functioning.
4. What are some causes of the problem?
5. What solutions have you already attempted to solve this problem?
6. What do you think will happen if the problem is not solved?
7. What are some constraints to a workable solution?

What did you think about this exercise? Were you honest in your answers to the questions? Were you able to answer all the questions or were there some questions you weren't able to respond to? Does this exercise change or modify how you see your problem? If so, how—for the better?

5.2 Brainstorming Solutions to the Problem

Now that you've analyzed this problem of yours, try to brainstorm five possible solutions. I know you've been over this a million times, but most likely you've proposed the same two or three solutions over and over. This time, get crazy. Brainstorm some wild and ridiculous ideas! Give yourself two minutes for this exercise. Here goes! List at least five possible solutions to this problem of yours (I'll supply the other five).

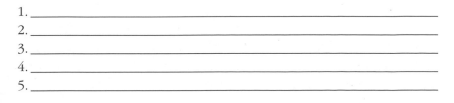

1. _____
2. _____
3. _____
4. _____
5. _____

6. Don't do anything for one year and see what happens.
7. Make the current situation worse by increasing the symptoms.
8. See the problem as an invitation to become a different kind of person.
9. Leave the situation/the state/the country.
10. Lose interest in the problem by creating a more serious problem in your life.

How did the brainstorming session go? Did you refrain from evaluating your solutions? Could you get a little wild and crazy in your suggestions? How did that feel to you? What do you think of your list? What do you think of the five solutions I suggested at the end?

5.3 Group Problem-Solving Activity

Have your group go through the first three steps of the standard problem-solving agenda—check-in, problem analysis, and brainstorming—to begin to solve a small, manageable problem facing the group. For example, your group can explore the following hypothetical problem: "What should be done about communication studies students who consistently talk in class while the instructor is speaking or students are delivering speeches?" Make sure each group member has a list of the questions in step 2 and receives instruction on the brainstorming technique. Good luck!

Preparing for Discussion

> The secret to success is to know something
> that everyone else doesn't.
>
> HENRY FORD

There's a story about a high-rise apartment owner who tried to get his broken furnace to work after it quit for the second time one winter. The owner hired three different furnace technicians to locate the problem. But each time the problem could not be solved. Finally, the owner phoned a fourth technician, who listened to his problem. The old technician guaranteed he could solve the problem.

"Are you sure?" demanded the young apartment owner.

"I think I've seen this problem before," assured the technician. "Most mechanics wouldn't know where to look, but I'm certain I can help you."

Later that day, the mechanic met the owner at the apartment high-rise. The owner led the old man down to the basement where the furnace was located. The furnace was a complicated maze of pipes, wires, and odd-shaped contraptions. The old man walked deeper into this jungle of sheet metal and piping. Eventually, the mechanic stopped, felt the metal above his head, and then selected a rubber hammer from his tool pouch. He gently tapped once on a small cylindrical box located above one of the thermostats.

Immediately, the giant heater grunted twice, then coughed up a deep roar of massive flames within the once-dark interior of the furnace. The fans began to swirl, pushing the heat up into the building. Within a minute, cheers could be heard from the tenants on the lowest floors, as the warm air flowed for the first time in days.

"You're a genius!" shouted the young apartment owner. "What will this minor miracle cost me?"

"The bill is $500," replied the mechanic.

"That's outrageous! You're charging me $500 for tapping a metal box just one time?" he screamed.

"Oh, no. The tap of my hammer was only $1," smiled the old man. "Knowing where to tap cost you $499."

Knowledge is power. The effectiveness of your group is determined to a large extent by the information it has at its disposal. The combined knowledge of the group is the material with which it will generate solutions that will solve the problems it faces. Many people will make no special effort to educate themselves about the problem their group is attempting to solve. But you can determine the amount of information you possess and contribute. This chapter will show you how to research for your group discussions and contribute information that will help you create a more effective group.

YOU DON'T KNOW EVERYTHING

No one knows everything. If we did, we wouldn't need the help of others to solve problems in the real world. The furnace technician knew how to fix the furnace, but he might not know how to balance the books. The apartment owner might know how to balance the books, but he didn't know how to fix the furnace. In fact, the first three mechanics didn't know how to locate the problem. Each person knows some things, but not everything about everything. You don't, and I don't.

> What we prepare for is usually what we get.
> WILLIAM SUMNER

Yet people like you and me will participate in a small group without ever once researching the problem, interviewing experts in the field, or even giving the issue any prior consideration or thought before taking our seat at the meeting.

Many times, we simply show up at the meeting, glance at the material sent to us by the chairperson, grab a cup of coffee, and settle down in our chair for another long discussion. I know this happens often. I've been guilty of it more than I'd care to admit.

Our lack of preparation is a result of many factors. We're too busy with other matters to devote any time to research. We might never have learned how to conduct library research or interview an expert. We're lazy. A million other things seem more appealing, like skiing, shopping, visiting, eating, gossiping, and sleeping. Even staring at the walls of our office with our feet on the desk would be better than researching.

WE CAN ALWAYS KNOW MORE

Ideally, a small group would be made up of individuals who are experts in the problem area they are examining. Yet, that is not practical. The majority of groups are made up of interested and concerned people like you and me. We want to get a candidate elected. We want to put a stop sign at the end of our street. We want to raise funds for a favorite charity. Or we just want to make our neighborhoods safer from crime.

No matter what we're trying to accomplish as a group, research can help us in our attempt to achieve the best solution. You won't necessarily have to make a trip to the public library, but you could phone around to see what other cities have done to reduce crime in their neighborhoods. You can conduct a series of brief interviews with a police officer, a Neighborhood Watch coordinator, a locksmith, and even an ex-thief to collect information and ideas that will benefit your group's attempts to make your neighborhood safer from crime.

Research is not only looking up information in your local library. **Research** is any activity that broadens or increases your information base on any topic or subject. In fact, some of your most helpful information will come from experts who deal with your group's problem every day of their lives.

No matter how much you know about the specific problem or issue confronting your group, you can always know more. The more information and evidence a group has at its disposal, the greater the probability its efforts will produce a solution that is workable and acceptable to all group members.

WHERE TO RESEARCH

The four primary sources for information about your group's topics are your own knowledge and experience, library research, interviews, and surveys.

Tapping Your Personal Knowledge and Experience

One of the most neglected areas of research is your own knowledge of and experience with the problem. Take a moment to sit in a quiet part of your house and close your eyes. Imagine a scene from the problem your group is researching. In the case of bicycle theft, what experiences have you had in this area? Has a bicycle of yours ever been stolen? Have your neighbors, friends, or relatives had their bikes stolen? What did you/they experience? What did you/they learn? What precautions do you/they currently take to reduce the chances of future theft? Do any books, television documentaries, magazine articles, or lectures related to this topic come to mind? Do any people having special expertise or interest in this topic come to mind?

As you reflect on your own experience and knowledge of the problem, keep notes with pencil and paper. Jot down any idea, thought, experience, or feeling that may provide information to the group's discussion. You'll be surprised by the amount of knowledge and experience you may already possess about the problem.

This activity of surveying your own knowledge and experience can also generate ideas on where to look for information and whom to seek for expert testimony. Let your mind wander as you research your own experience. Keep your mind open to discovering forgotten experiences and bits of information in the corners of your mind.

Using Library Resources

Any library, regardless of size, usually provides the following sources of information that you will need to research your topic.

The **card catalog** is an index of all the library's books by author, title, and subject. This catalog is your primary guide to the books in the library. If you are unfamiliar with its operation, ask the librarian for assistance.

Periodicals (magazines, journals, and newspapers) are another source of information for your research efforts. The *Reader's Guide to Periodical Literature* will be your most valuable resource for locating periodical articles related to your topic. Periodical information is generally more current than information provided by books and encyclopedias. The *Reader's Guide* indexes the articles of more than 130 American periodicals on a wide range of topics.

Your library should have **newspaper indexes** for your local daily in addition to the *New York Times Index*. Local newspapers will often provide the most valuable information concerning problems specific to your area. (Also consider contacting the local newspaper and explaining your research project. Newspaper folks are often helpful in assisting you in any way they can.)

Most libraries utilize computer technology to make your research easier, faster, and more comprehensive. **Computers** speed up your survey of books and periodicals. **CD-ROM technology** gives you access to vast quantities of information available from encyclopedias, periodicals, and newspaper indexes. If you are already familiar with computers, you know the speed, power, and enjoyment this technology provides. If you are not, don't be afraid to ask the librarian for some basic instruction on their use. A few minutes of computer instruction will open up a new world of information to you.

Internet

One of the most powerful tools you have to access information from all over the world is the **Internet**, a collection of computer networks that link computers from around the world. You literally have the collective knowledge of millions of organizations, groups, and people at your fingertips.

You have probably already used or will use the Internet to research a paper, check the stock market, or make reservations for a concert. The Internet can also be a fabulous source of information for researching your discussion topics. If you are unfamiliar with using the Internet, ask a librarian for help or enroll in an Internet class at your college. The few hours you invest learning how to use the Internet will produce countless benefits in the coming years.

Keep these two facts in mind when using the Internet. First, much of the information on the Internet lacks authority. Anyone with a computer and Internet access can post information, so some of the information you get will be outdated, misleading, or false. You need to evaluate the information with care. Some of the critical-thinking skills discussed later in this chapter will be helpful in analyzing what you find on the Internet. Second, many valuable sources of information are not available on the Internet, such as copyrighted books, encyclopedias, index and abstract services, and scholarly journals. Given this fact, you will still need to make a trip to the library when researching a discussion topic.

You will want to keep a series of questions in mind as you access and evaluate information from the Internet:

1. Is the author of the information a qualified expert in the field? What are the credentials of the author, organization, or agency posting the information?

2. Is the information accurate? Is the information consistent with your library research?
3. Is the information current? Are the sources up-to-date? If no date is given, the information may be old.
4. Is the information objective? Are sources cited? Are the conclusions based on fact? Are personal opinions and bias clearly stated?

Whatever Internet information you consider, you owe it to your group to present data from reliable, objective, and current sources. Subject your Internet information to the same standards you would library information. You don't want to share false or misleading information with group members.

Conducting Interviews

Although you may be reluctant to ask for an interview from a local expert, the rewards of doing so can go beyond those of gaining valuable information. Many a friendship, both professional and personal, and many a job have blossomed because of a fifteen-minute interview. Not only will you be gathering expert opinion regarding your topic of discussion, you will be given the opportunity to connect with a person you would have otherwise been a stranger to.

The first step in conducting an interview is to decide with whom you want to talk. If your problem is neighborhood crime, you may want to speak with the local police chief. If your topic deals with electing a local candidate, you may want to talk with a political campaign director.

After you decide on one or two experts to interview, the second step is to request an interview. Whether you request an interview in person, over the telephone, or in a formal letter, keep your request brief and friendly. Let the person know you would like to spend only fifteen minutes for the interview at his or her convenience (not yours). If the person cannot grant an interview, thank him or her for the time and try the next candidate. If the person agrees to the interview, great!

> Is there anyone so wise as to learn from the experience of others?
>
> VOLTAIRE

The third step is to write a list of questions for the interview itself. This should be done only *after* you have researched the topic from your own knowledge and experience and in the library. This preparation will enable you to ask more enlightened, specific, and articulate questions.

The fourth step is the interview itself. Be punctual. Nothing is more annoying to your interviewee than your arriving late to a meeting you requested. Dress up for the interview. Don't arrive in your T-shirt and old jeans. Stick to your time limit of fifteen minutes. At the end, thank the interviewee.

Finally, after you have returned from the interview, take a moment to write a brief thank-you card or letter to the interviewee. The few minutes and the cost of the stamp will add a touch of class that few interviewers ever consider.

Taking Surveys

For some topics, the attitudes and opinions of a group of individuals may provide valuable information and help in your decision-making efforts. A survey can gather information about the seriousness and nature of the problem, generate a list of potential solutions, or provide you with an idea of the support or opposition your solution will receive if proposed. These and many other uses suggest that surveys are a rich source of information for your group.

Whether it is randomly surveying twenty employees concerning their feelings on reducing medical coverage rather than cutting wages, or polling the neighbors on their feelings about lowering the speed limit in the neighborhood, the opinions of a group of people can be extremely informative.

If you decide to include a survey in your research, keep these suggestions in mind. First, develop a clear idea of what you are trying to achieve in your survey. Second, select a large enough population to be representative of the entire population being sampled. In some cases, the number of people affected by the problem is small so that you can poll all of them. Third, decide whether to interview people face-to-face, over the phone, or by mail. Fourth, construct a questionnaire that is to the point, is clearly written, and asks only what needs to be addressed. Finally, test the clarity of your survey in a pilot study or minisurvey.

For most discussions, your survey doesn't need to be too elaborate or statistically perfect. A simple polling of neighbors' attitudes or the collection of coworkers' opinions will be adequate. If a more complicated or involved survey is necessary, you may want to consult a book on survey methods or ask someone who has had previous experience in conducting surveys.

WHAT TO RESEARCH

Next, let's consider what to look for when you research. The items you want to seek information and evidence about are the questions from step 2 of your standard agenda—analyzing the problem (Chapter 5).

These questions focus on your research efforts. You should try to gather as much information as you can about these questions. The following are merely suggestions. Feel free to add to, modify, and delete from this list as you see fit.

What Is the Problem?

The group should agree on what the problem is and define it. Avoid vague, general descriptions of the problem. Be as specific as possible. For example, instead of "crime," your group might want to focus more specifically on "department-store shoplifting by pre-teenage children in Santa Clara County." This definition will focus the group's research and discussion much more than a general description.

> A problem well stated
> is half solved.
>
> CHARLES KETTERING

What Is the Question of Policy?

The group should agree on the question of policy before you begin researching the topic. Remember to begin the question of policy with "What should be done about . . . ?"

What Is the Nature of the Problem?

Find information describing the specific nature of the problem you are investigating. What exactly is the problem? What are the parameters of the problem? Are there any limitations or special conditions presented by the problem? How long has the problem existed? What is the history of the problem?

Whom Does the Problem Affect?

Determine who is affected by the problem. Does the problem affect primarily men, women, or children? Young or old people? Does the problem affect a specific subgroup? Try to get as much information about those affected by the problem as possible.

How Serious Is the Problem?

This is a question of value. Not all individuals will perceive the problem as being serious, but you need to establish some measurement of its magnitude, scope, and significance. Try to obtain statistical information describing the size and seriousness of the problem. Expert testimony on its seriousness is also helpful in determining how the group should address the problem.

What Are the Causes of the Problem?

This can be both a question of fact and a question of value. It is a question of value because experts may hold differing beliefs on the probable cause or causes of the problem. Your task is to obtain information on the problem's original cause or causes. Get as much information as possible, citing how and why the problem came into existence.

What Solutions Were Tried Already?

In your research, be on the lookout for solutions that have been attempted already to reduce or eliminate the current problem. Be as specific as possible when you describe solutions that have been previously attempted. Also list organizations and individuals who attempted a solution. Describe the effectiveness of their attempt(s) and discuss any suggestions the organizations and individuals may have for future attempts.

What Will Happen If the Problem Is Not Solved?

What do experts or the literature say will happen if this problem is not solved? Once again, this is primarily a question of value, because experts will have differing views. Describe as specifically as you can the situation or conditions that will result if the problem is not solved or its effects reduced.

What Are the Constraints for a Workable Solution?

Suggest at least three specific constraints for a workable solution to this problem. For instance, three criteria for a solution to the problem of reducing neighborhood theft may be that the solution must (1) cost less than $500 to implement, (2) be implemented within sixty days, and (3) involve participation by all residents. These constraints will help determine the merit of the solutions the group considers.

What Are Five Solutions That Satisfy Your Criteria?

After you have completed researching the problem (questions 3 through 9), brainstorm five solutions. You may want to brainstorm more, but try to keep it manageable. You will be sharing your ideas during the group's brainstorming session.

CONSTRUCTING AN INFORMATION SHEET

An easy method for recording all your research data is to use an **information sheet**, which contains the ten questions from your problem analysis and the evidence you gathered for each question. You should cite the author, source, and date for each piece of information you include, in case another group member questions your data. For an interview, cite the expert's name and qualifications, and the date of the interview. Here's an example of a question and the corresponding evidence and documentation for an information sheet.

> 6. What are the causes of the problem?
>   A. "Increased drug use is the primary cause of increased home robberies."
>   Police Chief Mark Henson, San Rafael Police. Interview, 8/26/03.
>   B. "The increase in home robberies is due to the increase in drug use."
>   Article by Sheila Graves, *San Rafael Times,* 8/18/03.

When you research the answers to the questions in step 2 of the standard agenda, you may need to refer to more than one kind of research source. Don't limit yourself to only magazines, newspapers, books, or expert opinions. Use as many sources of information as you can discover.

TESTING EVIDENCE AND REASONING

The purpose of researching the problem is to broaden the information base available to your group. Each piece of information or evidence added to the discussion increases the group's chances of discovering a workable and acceptable solution to the problem. Without the research of each group member, the probability of discovering a viable solution is decreased. Information is power.

During the group's discussions, members share information, especially during step 2 (analysis of the problem) and step 4 (discussion of the strengths and weaknesses of the better solutions). It is for the benefit of the group that members carefully examine the evidence, proposals, and the reasoning supporting the proposals. **Critical thinking** is the process of analyzing and evaluating information and ideas in order to reach sound judgments. Only with critical thinking can the group select the best solutions.

Three categories of research contributions require examination—opinions, evidence, and proposals. These are the three most prevalent contributions of researched information to group discussion.

Testing Opinions

Although personal opinions of group members are not technically documented information or evidence, they can often be presented as such without the expert testimony or evidence to support it. Examples of personal opinions stated as fact are:

> The rise in crime is due to the influx of minorities into our
> area.
> Juveniles are the cause of the increase in crime.
> The solution is more state and federal laws against drug
> addiction.

In each example, the personal opinion was stated not as an I-statement, but rather as a statement of fact or expert testimony. When you hear statements such as these in a discussion, you can force the speaker to own his statements simply by asking, *"Is this your personal opinion?"* Most of the time, the speaker will qualify his personal opinion by rephrasing his opinion, such as:

> *I think* the rise in crime is due to the influx of minorities into
> our area.
> *It's my opinion* that juveniles are the cause of the increase in
> crime.
> *I believe* the solution is more state and federal laws against
> drug addiction.

The importance of forcing I-statements is that the speaker cannot subtly persuade or influence the group with more credibility than his own opinion should carry. It also separates personal opinion from expert opinion during discussion. If the speaker doesn't own his opinion, but instead says, "It's my opinion and the opinion of others," or "Experts say the same thing," then ask, *"What evidence do you have to support your last statement?"* The purpose of asking for evidence is to examine the support for the speaker's statements.

The sharing of opinions is important to group discussion. With them, the group gets a feel for the attitudes and positions of each member. However, opinions need to be posed as I-statements. If members don't own their opinions, their statements can be mistaken for expert testimony or research findings, which can lend unwarranted weight to their statements.

Testing Evidence

In the course of discussion, especially during problem analysis, group members may present documented evidence. Most of the time, you'll jot down the information in your notes if you think it's important, thereby adding to the group's information base. But on some occasions a piece of evidence might sound contradictory to the rest of the information presented on the problem. Or the evidence may sound outdated or not as recent as you would like. Or you may want to know more about the author of the research, the publication, or source. If this is the case, then testing evidence is required. Testing the quantity, quality, recency, and relevancy of research presented during discussion is not only your right as a group member, it is also your responsibility. Let's briefly examine the four tests of evidence.

Testing quantity. The evidence or information a group member presents may be documented fully, with author, source, and date, but you may want to know if there is other supporting evidence. To base decisions solely on one study or one expert testimony may not be the wisest course of action. Other experts who agree with the testimony or research presented lend additional strength to the position. You can test for the quantity of evidence by asking such questions as: "Do you have *additional evidence* to support this point?" "Were there any *other studies* suggesting the same conclusion?" "Did anyone else find *similar evidence?*" By asking for supporting evidence, you also encourage low-verbal group members to contribute.

Testing quality. Group members may present reams of evidence supporting a certain point or position, but the quality of the sources or the qualifications of the authors or experts could be questionable. The second test of evidence is quality. You may need to know the source of the evidence, the qualifications of the author, or the specifics of the design of an experiment.

To test for the quality of evidence, the following questions can be helpful: *"What* is the source of your evidence?" *"Where* did you find that information?" *"Who* is the author of your evidence?" *"Describe* the qualifications of the author." These and other related questions can test the quality of the evidence presented during discussion. Don't be afraid to ask questions about the quality of evidence. Most people will readily provide the additional information you are seeking. An unwillingness to do so is also valuable for the group to consider.

Question Authority.

BUMPER STICKER

Testing recency. The more recent the evidence, the more valuable it can be to the group. Outdated or old evidence or information provides questionable value to the discussion. If a member cannot cite the date of an article or research finding, the evidence can be misleading or counterproductive if more recent and contradictory information has been discovered. That's why it's important to know the recency of evidence shared in discussion. Here are some questions that test for recency: *"When* was that evidence published?" *"How recent* is your information?" *"When* was the interview conducted?"

Testing relevancy. Evidence that is irrelevant to the discussion provides no valuable contribution to the discussion. The truth or falsity of irrelevant evidence doesn't concern the group, for it has no bearing on the topic being discussed. Often, irrelevant evidence or information isn't identified as such during discussion and the discussion gets sidetracked or even derailed. Silent group members who are reluctant to challenge the relevancy of such information may feel frustration and hostility. For the sake of the task and social dimensions of the group, you need to test the relevancy of evidence by questioning its bearing on the topic. Here are some ways to pose the question: *"How* does your evidence *relate* to our discussion?" *"What is the connection* between your evidence and the topic?" *"What is the relevance* of your evidence to our discussion?"

The four tests of evidence will improve the quality of group discussion. Without adequately testing questionable or unclear evidence, the information being considered can be confusing, misleading, and even harmful to the effectiveness and productivity of the discussion.

When testing evidence, keep four guidelines in mind. First, the purpose of testing information is clarification and thoughtful consideration, not personal attack or assault. Second, your nonverbal communication cues should match this intent of clarification. Be soft in your tone of voice. If the speaker is offended by your question and responds defensively, maintain your gentle nonverbal posture. Third, let the other person "save face." By this I mean give the person you are questioning some room to clarify, modify, or withdraw his information. Don't push the speaker. Don't attack the speaker. Simply pose your question and let her respond. Finally, submit your own evidence to the four tests before you enter the discussion.

Testing Proposals

The testing of proposals occurs when the group discusses the strengths and weaknesses of the better solutions. A proposal is stated in the form of a solution to the problem the group is considering. During the course of group discussion, many proposals will be presented for consideration. Effective group problem solving requires critical testing of these proposals.

A **proposal** is any solution the group is asked to accept or support. The **reason** is the rationale for accepting the proposal. The **inference** connects or links a particular reason to the proposal. These inferences can be either valid or invalid. The logical structure of any argument would look like this:

Because (reason) and (reason), therefore (proposal).

Here is an example of a proposal you might encounter in your group's discussions:

We should adopt a salary freeze if profits drop by 10 percent *(proposal)* because it has been successful in other companies *(reason)* and it involves the participation of all employees *(reason)*.

Or stated in logical structure form:

Because it has been successful in other companies *(reason)*, and *because* it involves the participation of all employees *(reason),* we should *therefore* adopt a salary freeze if profits drop by 10 percent *(proposal)*.

Very rarely will a proposal be stated with all its reasons. Usually someone will say, "I think we should freeze salaries if profits drop by 10 percent."

At this point in the discussion it's important to test the reasons supporting a particular proposal. The way you test is to ask for the reason or reasons supporting the proposal—"Let's examine the reasons supporting this solution." The inferences that link the reasons to the proposal are rarely stated; they are usually implied or suggested. Therefore, it is important to examine and test the validity of these inferences.

Inferences are either deductive or inductive. With a **deductive inference**, you begin with a generally accepted fact or belief and connect it to a specific issue to draw a specific conclusion or proposal. If the reasons are true, the proposal must be true. For example:

> *Because* all prison inmates must be at least eighteen years old *(reason), and* Bob is a prison inmate *(reason)*,
> *therefore,* Bob is at least eighteen years old *(proposal)*.

A deductive inference forces us to accept the conclusion. If the reasons are true, there is no chance that the conclusion is false.

An **inductive inference**, on the other hand, is one in which we project a likely or probable outcome or conclusion based on one or more known facts or experiences. The inductive inference does not force or guarantee the truth of the conclusion or proposal; it merely speaks to the probability of it being true. For example:

> *Because* Bob has already served his prison term *(reason), and* Bob has obeyed all the regulations of his probation *(reason), and* Bob has been attending church regularly *(reason),*
> *therefore,* Bob will never commit a crime again *(proposal)*.

The important thing to remember about inductive inferences is that they cannot guarantee the conclusions they suggest. They can suggest only a high probability of correctness or truth. In the example above, we cannot be 100 percent certain Bob will never commit a crime again, even though he served his time, obeyed the probation rules, and attends church.

Most inferences suggested in your group discussions will be inductive. In other words, you must test the validity and soundness of the reasons supporting each proposal. Here are some questions you can ask when testing inductive inferences:

> Are there *sufficient* reasons to accept the proposal?
> Are the reasons *directly relevant* to the proposal?
> Do we have *sufficient evidence* to support each reason?
> Is the *evidence* supporting each reason *acceptable, recent,* and *relevant*?

RECOGNIZING LOGICAL FALLACIES

In addition to testing the reasons supporting a proposal, you should be alert to any logical fallacies contained in the inferences suggested by each proposal. A **logical fallacy** is a mistake in logic or a mistaken or false belief. The most common logical fallacies you will encounter in your discussions are discussed below.

Overgeneralizing

An **overgeneralization** is a conclusion based on insufficient evidence. For instance, if there were two reports of car stereo thefts in your neighborhood during the past month, you might have concluded that the rate of car stereo thefts is on the increase nationwide. This conclusion is not supported by the data. Two reports of car stereo thefts in your neighborhood is insufficient evidence to make generalizations about the nation. When this happens in a group, you should inquire about additional evidence to support the conclusion or suggest that there is insufficient evidence to support the proposal or conclusion.

Causal Fallacy

A **causal fallacy** is an argument that suggests two events are causally connected, though no such relationship is established. This is one of the most common fallacies made in discussion. Someone says, "We've never had a problem with car stereo thefts until you moved into the neighborhood." The speaker has assumed that the presence of the new neighbor is the cause of the problem, which may or may not be

true. But a causal link has not been established. The speaker has provided no evidence showing that the new neighbor is the cause of the
problem.

If a causal fallacy is made, one approach you can take is to suggest
additional causes or causal relationships that may explain the event.
You can also mention that simply because these two events occur at
the same time, it doesn't necessarily follow that one causes the other.

False Analogy

A **false analogy** assumes that because two things are alike in one or
more respects, they are necessarily alike in some other respect. In
group discussion, a solution to a problem is suggested because that
solution worked somewhere else. Suppose someone draws the analogy between eating and marriage. Eating the same food day after day
would quickly become boring, he argues. Therefore variety in food
selection is desirable. Similarly, he concludes, having only one girlfriend can also become boring, so maintaining relationships with three
women at the same time would eliminate such boredom.

Do you see the fallacy of this analogy? What works under one
circumstance does not always work under another. If you believe a
false analogy is being used, question the strength of the similarities
of the two circumstances or situations. After careful examination,
are you convinced the two situations are similar enough to warrant
comparison?

Either-Or Thinking

The **either-or fallacy** supposes that only two options are available for
consideration and that one of them must be accepted by the group.
"Either we do it this way or we do it that way." "Either you support the
solution or you don't." "Either you are with the group or against the
group." Each statement gives only two positions for consideration,
when in reality, many positions are possible.

When either-or thinking happens, don't let your group be fooled
into believing they can take or consider only two positions. There are
always more. Challenge either-or thinking in your group by suggesting
other options or speaking in terms of more and less. For instance,
instead of describing a proposal as good or bad, you can point out that
it is less expensive than some and more practical than others. Don't let
the group's thinking become too rigid or limited.

Ad Hominem Argument (Attacking the Person)

The **ad hominem argument** consists of attacking the opponent in a personal way as a means of ignoring or discrediting her evidence or position, instead of focusing debate on the evidence or issue under examination. An example would be to say, "Your view of gun control can't have validity because you're a Democrat." The attack is leveled against the person's character, beliefs, or behavior as a means of diverting attention from the strength of her arguments and reasoning. When this occurs in a group, try to direct the discussion back to the issue or bring the attacker's behavior to the attention of the group.

This chapter explored ways to increase and use your knowledge about a specific topic. When you work in groups, your knowledge base and ability to critically examine the information and reasoning employed by the group will determine the quality of your decisions and create a more productive group. Whether you are sharing information with your group or examining and analyzing the information of others, remember to do so slowly, respectfully, and gently, because your communication behavior influences and shapes the behavior of others.

INDIVIDUAL AND GROUP EXERCISES

6.1 Interviewing an Expert

Select a problem of at least statewide importance that you feel strongly about, such as the rising cost of education, air pollution, hate groups on the Internet, child abuse, or rising gas prices. Construct a question of policy for the problem you have selected and brainstorm five possible experts who have specialized training and/or experience with this problem. Choose one of the five experts and schedule a fifteen-minute interview. Interview the expert, using questions 3 through 9 from the information sheet outlined in this chapter.

Whom did you select for your interview? Why did you select this person? How do you feel about the questions you asked? Discuss your overall effectiveness as an interviewer. What did you learn about the problem? What did you discover about yourself in this assignment?

6.2 **Group Research**

Have your group select one communication behavior that all group members feel they should improve. Listening, clarifying messages, summarizing ideas, resolving conflicts, and encouraging low-verbal members to contribute are some examples of these behaviors. Once a topic is selected, have each member independently research two library resources and interview one expert in an effort to gather information about this particular communication behavior. Meet as a group and have members share the information they gathered from the two library sources and the interview. Also have members share what they learned from their research experience.

6.3 **Case Study Research Exercise**

Mr. Billings is a twenty-seven-year-old, part-time community college instructor in Communication Studies. He has taught for five semesters as a part-time teacher and has received excellent evaluations from administrators, peers, and students, especially noting his warm, encouraging support of students. Currently Mr. Billings is teaching one small-group discussion class on Tuesday evenings and returned the midterm exam two weeks ago. Everything had been going fine in the class until last week.

Two older women from the class saw Mr. Billings kissing Karen in the parking lot as they were leaving for the night. Karen is a nineteen-year-old student who is also in the class. Karen, a straight A student, has been visiting Mr. Billings during his office hours for the past six weeks to talk about class assignments. The discussions have encompassed her recent breakup with a boyfriend and her feelings of inadequacy. Mr. Billings and Karen discovered they were attracted to each other and, as a result, have gone out on two dates during the past two weeks, but have not been intimate. The two older women confronted Mr. Billings after class the next week, saying that they felt he was "taking advantage of Karen" and that his behavior was "unprofessional." Mr. Billings said his personal life was none of their concern and they should mind their own business.

On a sheet of paper, write two statements about this case that discuss: (1) the ethical considerations, (2) the legal considerations, (3) the professional guidelines of instructor behavior, and (4) your personal opinions as a student. Share your statements with members of your group.

CHAPTER SEVEN

Guiding Discussion

If you don't know where you're going
any road will do.

BASHO

HANSEN IS A SPECK ON THE MAP about thirty miles southeast of Twin Falls, Idaho. My wife's uncle runs a cattle ranch just outside Hansen, right at the foot of the Sawtooth Mountains. Uncle Chuck's house is nestled in a sleepy little hollow, flanked on both sides by a year-round creek and shaded by a grove of willows.

Several years ago, my family and I spent four days at Uncle Chuck's. Time stands still at his ranch. It takes me two days just to unwind and slip into country time. Schedules there are governed by the rising and the setting of the sun. Folks talk slowly, with a deep richness, unhurried, and seemingly unaffected by this century. I like all this, up at Hansen.

But what I like best is watching Sheila and Ted, Uncle Chuck's two spirited border collies, keeping a hundred head of cattle moving straight on course during a cattle drive.

Border collies, I'm told, are the smartest cattle dogs in the world. A hundred cows can be packed into a tightly stuffed orb by one dog and moved almost effortlessly, like the shadow of a cloud rolling silently over the flowing landscape. The dogs dodge, dart, shove, and pack the cows into one obedient, single-minded mass of livestock, headed for an as yet unseen destination.

One rancher down the road from Chuck's went into a three-month depression when his border collie, Nick, died of old age. The rancher shed more tears over Nick's death than he did when his wife left him. At least that's what Uncle Chuck says, and Uncle Chuck doesn't exaggerate. In fact, he doesn't say much at all. That's why the last night we were in Hansen, Uncle Chuck surprised me with something he shared.

"Too bad our cattlemen's association didn't have some border collies to keep us in line," he lamented, as we sat on the back porch steps. "Seems like our association can't ever seem to agree on anything because we don't stick to the topic."

"Like those cows, maybe you need some help staying on track," I suggested.

"Yeah. And we might be dumber than cows. At least cows don't fight with one another," he smiled.

I smiled too as we listened to the water in the creek begin its journey to the sea.

This chapter will show you specific ways to guide the discussion of a group in the task and social dimensions of interaction. Strangely enough, your influence and impact on the discussion of a group is initiated more through asking questions and making guiding statements than stating your opinions and feelings. In addition to learning specific ways to guide the group's discussion, you will be introduced to some guidelines on being a more effective follower in a group. Without the willingness and ability to follow, there can be no effective leadership. Create more effective groups by learning to guide and follow.

GUIDING DISCUSSION TO A SHARED PATH

The funny thing about trying to keep five or six people on track during a discussion is that it is not as easy as you might think. One person will start the discussion with an idea, only to be interrupted by someone else, who begins to weave a second, unrelated thought or idea into the discussion, while two people chuckle at a humorous remark made by a third speaker. And the sixth member of the group is staring out the window, oblivious to the other three conversations.

Each person, it seems, has a different idea of where to go, what to do, and how to do it. Some members talk a lot; others don't. At times, each group member seems to be taking a separate path.

The initial task during any discussion is not solving a problem. That will come in its own time, if it is to come at all. The initial task of the group is to keep the discussion focused, coordinated, and on track in a supportive, open atmosphere. No matter how well informed, committed, and articulate each member might be, the group can wander aimlessly, like cattle without those border collies, if it cannot stay focused.

This chapter will show you specific ways to guide the discussion of the group to a shared path—like border-collie training, but with a higher calling in mind. You won't be as pushy and controlling as a border collie, but you will know the moves to keep the group on track during your discussions. These communication behaviors are called **guiding behaviors** because they keep the discussion focused and coordinate the participation and con-tributions of the individual group members in the most productive manner possible.

> One question, one gentle word, can change the course of a conversation and a life.
>
> ALFRED ADLER

The goal is for group members to discover a wide array of guiding behaviors that they can put to use during a discussion, depending on the situation, the mood of the group, and their particular inclination at any given moment. Although you can view these behaviors as a lead-ership task, every group member should be skilled at guiding the dis-cussion, not just the designated group leader. If every group member is aware of and skilled in the use of these guiding behaviors, then the overall group performance will be enhanced.

TASK GUIDING BEHAVIORS

Task guiding behaviors are intended to keep the discussion produc-tive, participatory, and on track. Kenneth Benne and Paul Sheats have proposed a list of task and social roles that enable us to get a clearer idea of what specific behaviors individuals can perform in groups. The following is a modified list of these behaviors. Six task guiding behav-iors that initiate and maintain a productive task dimension during the group's discussions are requesting information, providing information, clarifying information, guiding or summarizing discussion, analyzing, and negotiating.

Requesting Information

Requesting information from the group is an important function of every group member. It serves to broaden the information base of the group, initiate interaction when the discussion lulls, and encourage low-verbal members to contribute. Requesting information is a basic communication skill that invites others to communicate, participate, and contribute. Here are some examples of requesting information:

What do we think about . . . ? How do we feel about . . . ?
Does anyone have any information or evidence dealing
with . . . ? Did anyone interview an expert about . . . ? What
information haven't we shared yet?

The important thing to remember about requesting information is that
you are opening up the discussion to everyone again. This behavior
can often have an invigorating effect on a discussion that is needlessly
stuck on an overworked item. It can also serve to discourage a high-
verbal member from monopolizing a discussion.

Providing Information

Sharing evidence, information, or personal opinion is a vital behavior each
group member is expected to perform. Without the sharing of information,
there can be no discussion. You have thought about and researched the
topic before attending the meeting, so you are prepared to provide the
group with the fruits of your labor. Here are some ways to begin:

> Providing evidence/information
> My research shows . . .   I read that . . .   One study
> suggested . . .   During my interview with _____
> I learned that . . .   According to . . .   A recent poll
> concluded that . . .

> Providing opinion
> I think . . .   It's my opinion that . . .   I believe . . .
> I feel . . .   It's my understanding that . . .

If you researched the topic, you owe it to the group to share or provide as much relevant information to the discussion as possible. By
withholding or failing to share your information, you can prevent the
group from arriving at the wisest decisions and proposing the best
solutions. You could be holding the one piece of information the
group needs to succeed!

Clarifying Information

After a group member shares information, some confusion or question
may arise about the content or meaning of the statement. This is when
you need to clarify any ambiguous information. Here are some ways
you can initiate that process:

> Are you saying . . . ? Do you mean . . . ? Do I understand
> your research to suggest that . . . ? So, this tells us that . . . ?
> Another way to say this may be . . . ? Can we interpret the
> evidence to suggest . . . ? Would you repeat that?

The purpose of clarifying information is to ensure that the picture in the speaker's head is the same as or similar to the one you intended. Clarify any ambiguous information presented to the group. Take the time to ask questions. This is true for group discussion work as well as for your personal life.

Guiding and Summarizing Discussion

Guiding and summarizing discussion behaviors keep the discussion on the agenda, regulate participation, and announce time limits. Without these behaviors, the group can lose direction. Notice how powerful each of these behaviors is in guiding the group:

> Initiating the agenda
> > Let's define the problem.
> > Can we move onto brainstorming solutions?
> > I think we can move to the next step of . . .
>
> Maintaining the agenda
> > I think we need to return to the agenda . . .
> > We need to return to the topic of . . .
> > How does this relate to our agenda item?
> > We're off track. Can we get back to . . . ?
>
> Regulating participation
> > So, what you're telling us is . . . ? (regulating high-verbals)
> > Can you summarize your point? (regulating high-verbals)
> > What is your opinion, Mary? (encouraging low-verbals)
>
> Announcing time limits
> > Our meeting should last one hour. It will end at 2:30.
> > We have ten minutes left. Do we want to go to the next
> > > agenda item?
> > Our time is up; shall we table this until next time?
>
> Summarizing discussion
> > So far, we've heard three explanations. They are . . .

The brainstorming list of solutions are . . .
I'm hearing two schools of thought on this.
First . . . and second . . .

Analyzing Evidence and Testing Reasoning

As mentioned earlier, the need for careful and thoughtful analysis of evidence and reasoning is crucial. You need to be able and willing to analyze the evidence presented and test the reasoning of the proposals set forth. Here are ways you can analyze evidence and test reasoning:

Analyzing evidence
> Do you have additional evidence for this position?
> (testing quantity)
> What makes this researcher qualified? (testing quality)
> When was the article published? (testing recency)
> How does this relate to our topic? (testing relevancy)

Testing reasoning
> Have we looked at enough examples to explain this
> event? (testing overgeneralization)
> Are there other causes that would explain this event?
> (testing causal fallacy)
> Are these two situations similar enough to warrant
> comparison? (testing false analogy)
> Could there be other positions? (testing either-or fallacy)
> Are we analyzing issues or attacking personalities?
> (testing ad hominem attack)

Analysis of evidence and reasoning is the hallmark of critical thinking. I cannot overstate your responsibility to test the thinking and information of your group. Without diligent effort on your part in analyzing evidence and testing the reasoning of arguments, the group's effectiveness will be compromised. Discover the detective within you.

Negotiating

We all possess the capacity to suspend personal judgment and appreciate the benefits of different points of view. Negotiating is the skill of bringing differing parties to mutual agreement; you'll find this skill particularly valuable as the group gets closer to consensus. These negotiating skills are also helpful in settling minor conflicts and differences throughout the course of discussion. Here are some ways you can help in the negotiating process:

> Can we all agree that . . . ? Do we all think/feel . . . ? Is anyone opposed to . . . ? What things can we all agree to? Can we combine the strengths of these two proposals? Is this solution workable and acceptable to all of us? Can we all live with this solution for a period of time?

Your ability and willingness to negotiate and serve as a consensus builder will be one of the most important contributions to the success of the group. Try to see the beauty and strengths in all the ideas and proposals presented to the group. Be positive and constantly alert to any common ground—areas of agreement, common ideas, and similar beliefs—where your group can meet as one.

SOCIAL GUIDING BEHAVIORS

Social guiding behaviors are designed to establish and maintain healthy interpersonal relationships between group members. These behaviors encourage and preserve the social dimension during group discussion. They include encouraging, expressing feelings, harmonizing, and energizing. Each behavior is designed to ensure a friendly, supportive, and trusting atmosphere within the group.

Encouraging

Many times group members need encouragement to continue speaking, participating, or even remaining in the group. Encouragement fosters a caring, supportive group atmosphere. You can be encouraging to others by acknowledging their presence, agreeing with their statements, complimenting their behaviors, or reframing negatives into positives. Some things you can say to encourage others are:

> Acknowledging
> > I'm glad you're here today, Ingrid! I see your point, Seth!

> Agreeing
> > I agree with you, Frank. Your comment makes sense to me.

Complimenting
> I appreciate the handouts you prepared for us, Sarah.
> Your idea is wonderful!

Reframing negatives into positives
> Another way to look at this is _____. (positive interpretation)
> By pointing this out, you showed me some positive
> aspects, such as _____.

When you participate in a discussion, look for ways to encourage others. We all need encouragement and compliments. Discover the part of you that nurtures, cares, and supports others. It can also be an enriching experience for you, the encourager.

Expressing Feelings

Although your small group is not a therapy group, the expression of feelings and the acknowledgment of those feelings are essential to a healthy social dimension of any group. Whether it is to congratulate the group's successes or explore the group's interpersonal conflicts, the expression of feelings is crucial to the health and maintenance of the group. Here are some ways to encourage the expression of emotions:

> How are we feeling right now?
> Are you guys as frustrated as I am? Maybe we need a break.
> I love being in this group.

Many groups avoid expressing any emotion. They incorrectly believe such disclosure is inappropriate to the group process or a sign of weakness. Nothing could be further from the truth. Without some gauge to measure the social dimension of the members, the group will not know when to devote attention to resolving an interpersonal conflict, celebrate a task success, or merely take a much-needed five-minute break. Do what you can to encourage the expression of feelings within the group.

Harmonizing

Occasionally a disruption appears in an otherwise supportive and friendly group atmosphere. The tension or conflict between two or more members rises to a level that affects the group's task dimension effectiveness. Whether it is a disagreement over a substantive issue, hurt feelings due to an insensitive remark, or a minor feud between two individuals, the social dimension of the group is negatively affected. You should make some attempt to bring harmony back to the group. Here are some things you can say to reestablish harmony:

> Maybe the two of you can discuss this matter after the meeting.
> Let's not allow our feelings to get the best of us.
> Can you two disagree without disliking each other?
> We need to focus on the issues, not personalities.

Continued conflict needs to be brought to the attention of the group. To ignore or deny its existence would give the conflict more power to disrupt the social dimension. Therefore, the initial intervention is to bring the tension or conflict to the conscious awareness of the group. Then the individuals involved can strive to discover some way to disagree without disliking, punishing, or hurting one another. We will cover specific ways to deal with this in greater detail in Chapter 10. For now, however, you might want to try some harmonizing behavior when there is tension or conflict within the group.

Energizing

Working with other people in a small group can be psychologically, emotionally, and physically draining. Extended periods of time spent discussing, debating, and deliberating are taxing and can quickly deplete our energy levels and exhaust our enthusiasm. When you sense that the vitality of the group is slipping, you can try to energize the group by saying:

> We've done well so far and we only have a little ways to go!
> I think we're doing a great job!
> I know we can accomplish what we've set out to do!

There are no magic words you can chant or somersaults you can perform that guarantee bringing a group to life. But your attempt at energizing the group can be inspiring in and of itself. Enthusiasm is contagious! Choose to be the source of energy when the rest of the group is ready for a nap—you may be surprised at your impact on the group's enthusiasm.

BEING AN EFFECTIVE FOLLOWER

So far this chapter has emphasized taking an active role in guiding the task and social dimensions of group discussion. But you also have to know how to be an effective follower. Every member of the group cannot be guiding and leading the others all of the time. Chaos would result if everyone was trying to lead and no one was willing to follow. Use the skills in this chapter to guide and direct the flow of discussion when appropriate opportunities arise—not all of the time.

When your skills are not needed to help guide the discussion, be a willing participant and an effective follower for the group's leader. What specific attitudes and behaviors can help you be an effective follower?

Putting the group first. The focus of most people is on the self. How am I feeling? What am I thinking? How does that affect me? What do I want? What can I get? To be an effective follower, you must be willing to put the group first and yourself second. This is not forever, just for a period of time. If the individual members do not subordinate their personal goals and needs to those of the group, there is no effective group.

> Why is the sea
> the king of a hundred streams?
> Because it lies below them.
> Therefore it is the king of a
> hundred streams.
>
> LAO TSU

Start by asking yourself, "What is good for the group?" instead of, "What is best for me?" This subtle shift in focus and emphasis might be your first step toward being an effective follower.

Listening to others. After you have made the decision to put the group first, you need to know what the desires and needs of the group are. Pay attention to the discussion of the other group members. In other words, keep quiet and listen. My father always used to tell me, "You never learn anything new when you're talking," so one very obvious way to follow the discussion is to listen. You may just learn some new things. Be a receptive follower.

Discovering things to agree with. I have the hardest time working with a chronically disagreeable person, someone who must disagree with everything everyone says. The disagreeing person constantly searches for weaknesses in your ideas, flaws in your thinking, and objections to your proposals. People like that are the opposite of the team player. Not only are they out for themselves, they are against everyone else as well. These people help create groups that experience strife, exhaustion, and often failure.

You can be an effective follower by being on the lookout for ideas and suggestions you can agree with and support. Look for those aspects of the discussion that are going well. Don't always focus on the weaknesses and flaws of everything you hear. Discover things to which you can agree. Be a positive follower.

Whenever someone shares an opinion or suggestion that you strongly agree with, don't just sit there in silence, say something. It can be something simple: "I like that idea," "I think that's a good point," or "I agree with your idea 100 percent!" You may even want to compliment the individual whose idea or opinion you agree with by saying, "Silvia, I think you have a wonderful idea," or "Congratulations, Tomas! That's the best suggestion I've heard this entire meeting!" People need to hear confirmation and affirmation that their ideas or suggestions are shared by others. You can follow their lead by simply agreeing with the ideas and opinions of others. Be a verbal follower.

Volunteering to support the suggestions of others. In addition to voicing your agreement with the ideas and suggestions of others, venture forth and commit to supporting them in tangible ways. Not only can you agree with them, you can volunteer to "put your money where your mouth is" and help in some physical way to bring their idea or opinion to fruition. Volunteer to do something to support their belief or suggestion by stating, "I'll do some research on the Internet for you," "I'll make the arrangements for the luncheon," "I can call those four managers and get their opinions if you'd like," or "Let me contact the personnel office and see what the policy is regarding your wonderful suggestion." Talk is cheap; volunteer your time and effort to support the ideas and suggestions of others. Be a helpful follower.

Rather than suggesting specific ways to show your support, ask people what is the most effective way you can help to advance their idea or suggestion. Simply inquire, "What can I do to support your suggestion?" "How can I help you advance this idea to management?" or say, "Count me in on implementing this solution." Many times people will know the best process or procedure to implement their idea or suggestion. Let the idea originator tell you how you can best serve. Let that person be the boss while you concentrate on being the follower who asks helpful questions.

Following through. Once you have been assigned a responsibility or given a task to support someone's idea or suggestion, you need to follow through. Be good on your word. Keep your promises. If you say you will do something, just do it. If you don't keep your promises, you not only let down the group, but you also jeopardize or destroy your reputation in the group as someone who can be trusted. Once you have agreed to something, complete the task. Your good name is at stake.

Being cheerful. Above all else, choose to be cheerful as you follow others. Don't go about your tasks and responsibilities with a grudging attitude or negative spirit. This type of behavior will harm the group's spirit and effort. It is better to withdraw from a group than be a source of resentment and ill will. Take your pity party somewhere else and sulk. So, do you promise to be cheerful while following the ideas and suggestions of others?

> Choose to be happy. It's one way to be wise.
>
> COLETTE

Good! A happy, cheerful attitude will bring joy and productivity wherever it goes. Be a cheerful follower, above all else.

You can have a more positive and productive impact on your group by encouraging others to participate and contribute, rather than always focusing on sharing your ideas and opinions. Asking guiding questions and making guiding statements are just two of the specific ways you can guide group discussion in the task and social dimensions of interaction. Being a willing follower is just as essential to creating an effective group as guiding the group, so realize that leading and following are simply two sides of the same process—creating an effective group.

INDIVIDUAL AND GROUP EXERCISES

7.1 Guiding Behavior in Your Personal Life

Use one or two of the task guiding behaviors from this chapter and implement them in your relationships with others. For instance, ask people more questions (requesting or clarifying information), compromise your positions (negotiating), or think more critically (analyzing). How does using these guiding behaviors feel in your daily interactions with those individuals in your life?

7.2 Guiding Behaviors in a Small-Group Meeting

Hold a twenty-minute meeting with a group of five classmates to plan a hypothetical class picnic. During the meeting, decide where the picnic will be held, how long the picnic will last, what to bring, who will bring what, and who will clean up. Also, come up with a list of six fun class activities or games, choose who will lead each game, and determine what prizes should be awarded. Your group will perform all of these functions and the rest of the class will simply come and enjoy the event your group has planned.

During the twenty-minute planning meeting, each of the five group members takes a turn at guiding the task dimension of the discussion for four minutes. After all five members have led the discussion, take a few minutes to share your reactions and give feedback to one another about their strengths and weaknesses.

7.3 Learning to Follow

This exercise will teach your body (not your mind) how to follow another person. The object of the exercise is for you to simply follow your partner's finger with yours for three minutes.

Choose a partner and sit comfortably in chairs facing each other, close enough so that your knees almost touch. Your partner raises her right index finger above her knees to about eye level and points it in your direction. You raise your left index finger to within one or two inches from her finger. For three minutes, your partner moves her finger within the two-dimensional plane between you (pretend that a sheet of glass extends from the floor to above your heads between your knees), and you try to follow it. No matter where your partner goes with her finger, you simply follow it as best you can. Your partner is not to move so quickly that it's impossible for you to follow. Neither of you is allowed to talk during the three minutes. Just see what it's like to simply follow her finger.

What was this experience like for you? Do your responses to this exercise give you any insight into your willingness and ability to be a follower in your group work? How can you modify or change your attitudes and behaviors to be a more effective follower in the future?

CHAPTER EIGHT

Leading a Group

A good leader makes opportunities
for others to succeed.

MAXWELL JOHNSTON

Fran didn't look like a leader to me. She was petite, about five feet tall, and weighed maybe 95 pounds. Her voice was soft, and when she took her seat at the conference table during the group's initial meeting, she appeared to be a head lower than the rest of us.

Fran was a new faculty member, clearly one of the youngest in our group. She looked almost like a student sitting at that oversized, wooden table in the conference room. The seven of us had been appointed by the president of our college to propose ways to market our institution to the local community.

There was no proposed agenda and no designated leader. Only the seven of us scheduled to meet eight times during the semester. Six of us knew each other from years past, but we didn't know Fran. However, during the following decade, Fran was going to become very well known to us—she would become our college president.

What makes an effective leader? Well, it depends. Each task and every group are different. What works in one setting may not work in another. But some common denominators are characteristic of an effective small-group leader. I observed them in Fran's interactions with us in that committee many years ago.

Fran's foremost purpose in every meeting was to serve the committee, not to further her own agenda, ideas, or proposals. She brought out the best in each of us by consistently demonstrating those guiding skills and behaviors discussed in Chapter 7. Fran would gently guide us back on track when we wandered, summarize the various points when we got long-winded, and negotiate consensus when we hovered

121

near agreement. She prepared handouts and visual aids for the group and even brought doughnuts to a meeting or two.

All these things she did without fanfare—without requiring the lime-light or special thanks, without our becoming jealous of her skills, without really anything. Although other members brainstormed better ideas or debated with greater skill, it was Fran who consistently and unselfishly brought out the best in each of us. She sincerely and deeply wanted the best for the group.

The effective leader is the one who serves the group well and helps the group realize its goal.

You can participate in the leadership of any small group. Leadership is not relegated to only one individual in a group; the leadership functions often can be shared by all the group members. You can create productive and successful meetings by using the suggestions outlined in this chapter and you can really enable the group to be effective by assuming the role of servant leader. The leadership skills you develop in this chapter will help you create effective groups.

WHAT IS LEADERSHIP?

Since the beginning of time, people in groups have listened to the counsel, followed the suggestions, and even looked up to specific individuals within the tribe, hamlet, community, or organization. These individuals are the leaders of the group. Whether inherited, won by battle or election, or arrived at by group consensus, leadership has been a focus of attention and interest throughout history. For the purposes of this book, however, discussion is limited to the leadership of small groups assigned to solve a problem.

> Everyone leads. Leadership is action, not position.
>
> DONALD MCGANNON

First, what is a leader? A **leader** is an individual who is perceived by group members as having a legitimate position of power or influence in the group. The leader can be assigned or designated to that position. Or the leader may emerge from within the group's interactive process or even by group election.

Leadership, however, is different. **Leadership** is the process of influencing the task and social dimensions of a group to help it reach its goal. By this definition, leadership can involve more than one individual. All group members can share leadership. Each individual in the group has the potential and opportunity to participate in the leadership functions of the group. Although this chapter provides specific and practical suggestions for a designated leader to more effectively run a meeting or manage a small group, it also emphasizes ways each group member can help the group reach its goal.

APPROACHES TO LEADERSHIP

To enhance your ability and willingness to participate in the leadership of small groups, you may find it helpful to examine the four most prevalent approaches to studying leadership: trait, styles, situational, and functional.

Trait Approach

The **trait approach** suggests that individuals are born with certain personality traits that make them good leaders. In the past, physical traits such as attractiveness, height, a deep voice, and a full head of hair were linked to or perceived as predictors or requirements for leadership. Personality traits such as achievement orientation, self-confidence, intelligence, enthusiasm, adaptability, sociability, and responsibility were also perceived as required traits for leaders. The trait approach implicitly suggests that most of these traits are characteristics an individual is born with. Thus, the "born leader" illustrates the trait approach to understanding why certain individuals become leaders. Television, movies, and the media often portray corporate and national leaders as individuals who possess these physical and personality traits, but in reality there are scores of famous leaders, and I'm sure you know of leaders in your personal life, who do not possess all the physical and psychological requirements set forth by the trait approach. Group process is too intricate and diverse, and personality too complex, to be so easily explained.

Styles Approach

The **styles approach** to leadership examines how an individual leads rather than why a certain individual becomes a leader. The three styles of leadership are autocratic, democratic, and laissez-faire.

Autocratic leadership. The **autocratic leader** rules with firm control over the group process. These leaders generally see themselves as the leader and the rest of the group as followers. Often, they will listen to the ideas and suggestions of the other group members or subordinates, but the ultimate decision-making process rests more with them than with the group. Autocratic leaders believe they know what is best for the group and expect the others to follow and support what they feel is the wisest course of action. Autocratic leaders will often use a variety of methods to enforce their decisions and establish compliance within the group.

Democratic leadership. The **democratic leader** encourages the full participation of group members in discussion and decision making. Democratic leaders recognize the value of group input and participation, and seek the majority opinion, or consensus. Emphasis is placed on the group, and democratic leaders lead by example, not by force.

Laissez-faire leadership. The **laissez-faire leader** lets the group lead itself. Leaders select this style because they are uncomfortable leading others or believe that their leadership will have counterproductive effects on the group. Operating from a "hands-off" approach, laissez-faire leaders generally see themselves as just another group member and will not attempt to enforce or exercise their position as leader. Instead, they let group members engage in the work themselves.

These three styles of leadership have advantages and disadvantages. Research has shown that the autocratic and democratic styles to leadership can be the most productive. The autocratic style produces more efficiently run groups, which complete tasks in less time. Groups under the democratic style generally produce the greatest member satisfaction, but require more time to complete tasks. The laissez-faire style is effective with extremely independent or creative group members who require a great deal of freedom and latitude to perform.

Current research on group productivity and member satisfaction confirms the notion that the democratic style of leadership appears to be the most effective (Schultz, 1996). I have found this to be true from my own experience. Keep in mind that the leader's communication skills and relationship with group members are important determinants of group success, regardless of leadership style.

Situational Approach

The **situational approach** to understanding leadership stresses that the requirements for effective leadership depend on the actual circumstances.

In the situational approach, groups locate the relevant characteristics of the situation and determine what kind of leadership style and personality would be the most effective in achieving the specific goals.

Paul Hersey and Kenneth Blanchard (1988) have proposed a very useful situational model for understanding leadership. They consider three very important variables:

1. The *amount of guidance and direction* (task dimension) the leader provides.
2. The *amount of interpersonal support* (social dimension) the leader provides.
3. The *readiness level* in performing the tasks that followers demonstrate.

The interaction between these three variables will determine which style of leadership would be most effective for a given situation with a particular group of people.

Hersey and Blanchard describe four leadership styles that are most effective for various situations. The **telling style** (high task/low social emphasis) is authoritarian and directive. This leader provides specific directions and close supervision, and puts relatively little effort into developing the social dimension of the group. The **selling style** (high task/high social emphasis) stresses authoritarian leadership with attention to the social dimension of the group. This leader attempts to convince or persuade the group that his or her decision or plan is the best, but it is still the leader's decision, not theirs. The **delegating style** (low task/low social emphasis) is laissez-faire or nondirective. The leader lets the group direct itself by giving members the responsibility to make decisions and implement solutions to problems. The **participating style** (low task/high social emphasis) is also laissez-faire. The leader lets the group make its own decisions and implement solutions, but will actively encourage the development of the group's social dimension.

The readiness level of group members is an essential factor in determining which style of leadership would be most effective. Readiness is determined by the ability and willingness of group members to perform the tasks needed to create and implement solutions. The ability is the knowledge and skills that group members bring to a particular task. The willingness is the group's motivation and commitment to accomplish the task.

When group members are at lower levels of task readiness or willingness to perform, the group is most effective when decisions are leader-directed. When the group members are at higher levels of task readiness or willingness to perform, the group decisions can be member-directed. The general rule is that the higher level of group readiness, the lower level of leader-directed decision-making.

Functional Approach

Whereas the situational approach stresses the readiness levels of the group members in both skill and willingness, the **functional approach** examines the communication behaviors of group members that help the group achieve its goal. Beatrice Schultz defines functional leadership as "a process in which a leader engages in many behaviors, both verbal and nonverbal, to help a group achieve a goal." Rather than paying attention to the characteristics of the leader, the style of leadership, or the situation within which the leader must emerge, the functional approach focuses on the individual acts that influence the task and social dimensions of the group and move the group toward its goal.

Will Schutz has proposed the "leader as completer" perspective on functional leadership. When group members fail to perform the necessary duties, the elected or designated leader has to do whatever it takes to complete the job. The duties are usually task dimension behaviors such as giving information, asking for information, guiding discussion, arranging for meeting times, or calling group members, but they can also include social dimension behaviors such as relieving tension or encouraging.

The functional approach to leadership I propose is that *every group member can help lead.* Although an elected or designated leader can arrange the meeting dates and times, plan the agenda, and initiate discussion, all group members carry out the task and social dimension behaviors of leadership.

During the discussion itself, the most vital behaviors that all group members can perform are the task and social guiding behaviors that were highlighted in Chapter 7:

1. Requesting information
2. Providing information
3. Clarifying information
4. Guiding and summarizing
5. Analyzing
6. Negotiating
7. Encouraging
8. Expressing feelings
9. Harmonizing
10. Energizing

Every group member can perform these guiding behaviors. During the meeting, the responsibility of participating in and guiding the direction of the discussion is not limited to the elected or designated leader. It can be shared by all group members. This modified perspective of the functional approach—every group member can help lead—is one that greatly enhances and encourages the participation of each group member. It also takes much of the pressure off the designated leader, because every group member is now encouraged to perform these vital tasks. Perhaps the most important advantage to this approach is that it empowers each member to see the entire process of group discussion in an entirely new light—one of greater ownership in both the process and the outcomes. No longer is just one individual able and willing to participate and guide the group at the leader level, but every group member is capable of completing the task.

SERVANT LEADER ATTITUDE

As you use these ten leadership skills, it's important to develop the attitude of the servant leader. Just like Fran in the opening story, the most effective leader doesn't sit back and bark out orders and commands, but rather participates and serves others. Rather than looking down from some glass-and-steel corner office watching group members labor, the effective leader is one of the group, participating equally with other members and oftentimes volunteering to do humble and menial tasks. Like Fran, the servant leader not only guides the meeting, but also is willing to buy the doughnuts on the way to the meeting and set up the chairs before the others arrive. There's a famous story

> Leading well means
> serving well.
> VAN CUMMINGS

about the chairman of Toyota Motor Company, whose desk was just one of many desks in the accountants division office. He always emptied his own wastebasket at the end of the day, just like the other workers in the area.

To be an effective leader, you must assume the attitude of a servant—one who creates opportunities for others to work well and realize their potential as human beings. It is a higher calling than that of the traditional leader who receives preferential treatment and respect and is served by others.

For thirty years, Robert Greenleaf was the director of management research for AT&T. He studied thousands of managers and corporate leaders in America and discovered that the most effective leaders "put serving others, including employees, customers, and community, first." It was Greenleaf, in his book *Servant Leadership,* who coined the term "servant leadership," which stressed the "leader's desire to serve first" as the most essential element in effective leadership.

Greenleaf discovered that the most effective leaders gave special treatment to their workers and subordinates without expecting it in return. He found that the most effective leaders "helped consensus evolve within the group" rather than shape or direct it. More striking, Greenleaf discovered that they "were sensitive to and encouraged the personal growth of their workers," and were not always focused on productivity, efficiency, and profits. Here are some suggestions that Greenleaf encouraged leaders to consider as they prepared to lead.

Be aware. Many leaders are so self-absorbed with their own needs and desires that they fail to be aware of the needs and desires of others. As a servant leader, you need to be aware, awake, and sensitive to the rest of the group as well as to yourself. You need to observe others, ask questions, open up, and be sensitive to others. This requires that you pay attention to what they do, what they say, and what they don't say. Equally important, you need to be aware of yourself—not just your conscious needs and desires, but those voices within you that are often drowned out by the noises and distractions of everyday living. Five or ten minutes of silently sitting each day can do wonders for increasing your self-awareness. Increased self-awareness will enable you to better serve others.

Listen. The most important communication skill a servant leader can use is that of listening. The servant leader, above all else, listens to what others have to say. How else can you find out what they need? Not only is listening essential to receiving messages, it also acknowledges and honors the person speaking. There is no more powerful way to communicate respect for other people than to keep your mouth shut and truly listen to their ideas, opinions, and feelings.

Be empathetic. The servant leader must feel what others feel. As a leader, you need to move beyond your own ego and see and feel the world through the eyes of others. Without the willingness and ability to be empathetic, you will lack the sensitivity and awareness to experience group members in a fuller, three-dimensional way. The process of maturity, not only for the leader, but for all people, is to move from self to others—the willingness and ability to get out of your own head and heart and experience the world from the vantage point of others.

Encourage the growth of others. The ability to communicate with others, to work with others, to resolve differences and conflicts with others, to compromise with others, to forgive others, and to celebrate with others are all activities of the small group. They are also important activities of personal growth. What group members learn and practice in the group also influences, shapes, and determines how they will live their lives when they get home. As a servant leader, you need to be sensitive to and encourage each member's personal journey to wholeness—to where they can communicate and experience their lives to the fullest. That is one of your most sacred responsibilities as a leader: to encourage each member's personal growth and development.

As a servant leader, lead a meeting in a way that creates effective and productive outcomes.

LEADING AN EFFECTIVE MEETING

One of the most important functions of any leader is to lead an effective meeting. Many specific skills and behaviors go into running a meeting that is productive, organized, and even enjoyable. After you decide to become a leader, use the following suggestions to help you prepare for, begin, and lead an effective meeting.

Deciding to Lead a Group

You must first decide whether you want to lead. Before you volunteer, are appointed, or are elected as the leader of a group, consider what it means to be the leader.

Clarify the leader's job description. Start by clarifying the duties and responsibilities of the position. Consult your boss, supervisor, group, or an appropriate source to review what is expected of you as leader. Get the job description in writing if possible. What are the expected time lines for projects? When does the position end? Under what circumstances can you be replaced? What special things should you know about your duties, the group members, or the project you will be in charge of?

Consider if you want to be the leader. Take the next two days to weigh the pros and cons of being the leader of a specific group. After considering the duties, responsibilities, and time expected of you, be honest with yourself. Is it something you really want to do? Is it something you really need to do? Is it a way to receive recognition or exercise power? Consider your motives. Ask yourself whether it is a position in which you would want to serve others—the group members and the organization.

If you've never led a group before, don't be afraid to accept the position or nomination. Every great leader had a first leadership position. This could be yours! If you decide to accept the position, you will discover many wonderful things about yourself and others. You may also experience moments of disappointment, stress, failure, and disillusionment. All this comes with the territory.

Preparing for the Meeting

Before you actually call the group to a meeting, there are several things you can do to prepare. Completing the following items before each meeting will help you create successful meetings.

Determine when to meet. Obviously, your group needs to meet. Usually, the meeting times and dates are determined for you. But if they're not, you need to contact group members and negotiate meeting times and dates.

After the scheduled meetings have begun, you may occasionally decide that a future meeting does not require members' physical presence, and that the information or business can be communicated or conducted by message or memo. Take every opportunity to conduct the group's business in the most expedient fashion possible. Use the phone, fax, e-mail, and interoffice mail to your advantage. If you decide not to convene a meeting, your group members will love you for it.

Prepare and send the agenda before the meeting. Prepare and send the meeting agenda (and any pertinent reading material) to each group member one week *before* the meeting. This gives ample time for group members to read, consider, and even research appropriate material before you meet. I usually have a rule when I chair a group that members cannot verbally participate in discussions if they haven't read the agenda *and* other material *before* the meeting. This prevents members from shuffling paper and reading material during discussion.

The following is an example of a generic meeting agenda. Refer to it when constructing your own agenda:

AGENDA

1. Call to order.
2. Approve agenda.
3. Approve minutes from previous meeting.
4. Announcements.
5. Reports (officers and committees).
6. Old (unfinished) business. List all items that will be before the group for discussion or action.
7. New business.
8. Adjournment.

When you construct the agenda, limit the number of items you schedule the group to address and discuss. I know a group leader who limits each meeting to one item or issue, not two or three—just one. He swears by this method. It's a little extreme, but I would rather err in his direction than have too many agenda items. A group needs focus, so limit the number of discussion items in new and old business.

Next, prioritize your agenda items, starting from the most important in terms of significance to the least important. That way, if your group doesn't get to the last item or two, at least you have addressed the higher-priority items. The rest can be the higher-priority items at the next meeting.

Before the Meeting

There are several simple things you can do before the meeting to put yourself and others in a positive frame of mind, focused and ready for the meeting.

Envision what will happen at the meeting. Before the meeting, take a few moments and try to envision what will happen. Close your eyes and visualize each group member at the meeting. See as many details of this mental picture as possible. Keep your eyes closed. Relax. Get a sense of what you want to happen.

Arrive early. Arrive ten to fifteen minutes early to the meeting. Arrange the chairs in a circle, check the lighting, open windows if it's stuffy, and plug in the coffeemaker. No, a secretary or assistant isn't supposed to do this—remember, effective leadership means effective service. Get a feel for the atmosphere of the room before people begin arriving.

Mingle with members. As the group members arrive, mingle, join in, and make them feel welcome. Thank people individually for coming early. Listen to them and be really present in mind and body.

Running the Meeting

Once group members have arrived, you can begin the meeting. These suggestions will help facilitate both the social and task dimensions of the group, and encourage a successful outcome to the meeting.

Start the meeting on time. About two minutes before the scheduled meeting time, announce to group members that the meeting is about to begin. Invite them to get another cup of coffee and then move to your seat. After they see you seated, they will usually follow. *Begin the meeting exactly on time!* This is the first official act you perform at each meeting. Don't be sloppy or indecisive with this initial responsibility.

Conduct a check-in. Let each member of the group check in by sharing one good thing that has happened since the group last met. Limit each member's comments to twenty seconds. This check-in provides each person with the opportunity to say something positive, reduces any speaking anxiety, and lets members know what's going on in one another's lives. Don't let members interrupt during a member's check-in. This will sidetrack the discussion. Just provide a brief time for the group members to say hello and get comfortable before making your announcements.

Make announcements quickly. After everyone is seated, get any announcements that weren't included in the agenda out of the way as quickly as possible. Announcements are not open to debate or discussion. Briefly answer any questions that arise. This is not the time to get bogged down with tangential remarks and off-the-track discussions.

State the meeting objectives and time limits. Thank group members for attending the meeting and for being punctual. Then state the objective or objectives for the meeting. Provide a tentative time limit for each objective or agenda item, and state the ending time for the meeting. Group members appreciate a leader who will publicly announce time limits for agenda items and the ending time of the meeting. It gets things out in the open and provides a framework for discussion.

Don't stop the meeting for latecomers. Occasionally, a group member will arrive late to the meeting. Don't recap what's already been covered and don't acknowledge or listen to excuses for being late. Simply continue the discussion without paying attention to the latecomer. Chronic tardiness can be a symptom of passive-aggressive behavior (indirect anger directed at you or the group) or a challenge to your power. Don't give the chronic latecomer any power.

Restate objectives and time limits periodically. About every ten minutes, restate the objective the group is currently working on and how many minutes are left in the meeting. If possible, avoid holding any meeting for more than sixty minutes. Human beings get tired and bored after one hour.

Remain impartial. As the leader, your primary goal is to ensure the smooth functioning of the task and social dimensions of the group. Let all group members voice their opinions on a particular issue before you share your thoughts. Your job is to serve the group by soliciting and guiding its discussion so that it stays on track and on time.

Guide the group. The specific guiding behaviors you can draw on to guide group discussion are discussed in detail in Chapter 7. Keep a note card summary of these guiding behaviors in front of you during each meeting as a reminder.

Seek participation. Requesting information is an important guiding behavior. Ask for the opinions of low-verbal members who have not contributed and summarize the long speeches of high-verbal members. Your group needs to know and experience your control of the group. They need to see that you are attempting to seek participation from everyone in the group. Be sensitive to who's not talking and who's talking too much.

Summarize often. Occasional summaries can work wonders to focus discussion, to quiet high-verbals, and to keep the group on time. Look for opportune moments to summarize ideas and progress.

Compliment members often. See the positive in the contributions and participation of each member. Verbally compliment individuals during the meeting. Someone once said, "A person can accomplish a great deal if he doesn't worry about who gets the credit." Don't worry about who ultimately gets credit for anything the group does. Give the credit (and compliments) liberally to your group members. You will not only boost their feelings of importance, but also encourage participation and encourage member loyalty to you.

Keep the meeting moving. Don't get bogged down on any one item or issue for too long. Table items to the next meeting if additional information is required or if the tension in the group is getting too great. Remember to summarize and state the time remaining in the meeting. During the last ten minutes, I usually give time-remaining announcements a couple of times: "We've got nine minutes left," "We've got six minutes left," and so on.

Conduct a check-out. During the last two or three minutes of your meeting, you may want to let the members check out by individually sharing one thing they liked about the meeting and one thing they think would improve the next meeting. Limit each member's remarks to twenty seconds. This check-out time can be very valuable for letting members compliment one another or the group and to provide specific suggestions for improvement. Remember to record any suggestions for improvement.

End the meeting on time. If you conclude the meeting on time, you will be establishing one of the most powerful norms of group work: "This leader ends when she says she will end, so I'd better get what I want to say in and accomplish what I intend to accomplish during the time or I'll have to wait until the next meeting." Stated another way, the norm you establish is *"This leader keeps promises."*

End the meeting on time and your group members will love you for it. Each member has a life outside the group (at least, you hope they do). So end on time and let them get on with their lives. During the last minute or so of each meeting, I summarize the objective or objectives we've accomplished and remind members of the next meeting time and date.

TAKING CARE OF YOURSELF AS THE LEADER

The duties and responsibilities of a leadership position can be psychologically taxing, emotionally fatiguing, and physically draining. Whether you're the president of a large corporation or the head of the Little League pancake breakfast, the job of leading a group of people can push you to the limits of your capabilities and patience.

To avoid leader burnout, I'd like to suggest some ways to take good care of yourself when you're the leader of a group. These are attitudes you can adopt and things you can do to remain centered, open, and productive in your role as leader.

Leave some things to others. Volunteer or accept a position of leadership only for a group whose purpose you believe in deep in your heart. Life will go on without you as the leader, so don't feel obligated to volunteer for a leadership position you don't believe in.

If you really don't believe in and support the functions and purpose of the local Little League, don't volunteer to chair the pancake breakfast committee. You can serve as a committee member out of a sense of obligation if your child or brother is on a team, but don't volunteer to chair the committee if your heart is not in it.

> Your number one responsibility is to take good care of yourself.
> S H E L D O N   K O P P

I realize sometimes you may not have a choice, such as at work, where a boss or supervisor assigns the responsibilities of leadership to you. In those instances, you can still choose to discuss your concerns or misgivings with your boss. Maybe you will be successful in changing your boss's mind. If not, choose to utilize the skills and understanding you gained from this book and lead with a positive attitude.

Leave your ego at the door. As the leader of a group, you will often be the target of criticism when things go wrong, the butt of jokes behind your back, and the last one to know if members are dissatisfied with your performance. In extreme instances, individuals and coalitions within your group can assail your recommendations, find fault with your style of leading, and attack your character. The price of leadership can be high.

You will need to discover ways to detach from your ego if you are to be an effective leader. Once you enter the meeting room, leave your ego at the door, or forever be pulled and tugged, hurt and angered by every questioning remark and critical suggestion directed toward you during the heat of discussion. Remember that you are not paid to be their friend. Your role is to lead.

Leave time for other things. Obsession is one of the most common mistakes leaders make. They do nothing but eat, think, and sleep their role as leader. The leadership position consumes their days and haunts their nights. To avoid this, make sure you leave time in your daily life for other things. Talk with family and friends about anything other than your task. Take up a new sport or hobby. Spend more time with your loved ones doing things you meant to do last summer. See more matinee movies during the week. Take walks around the neighborhood and make some new acquaintances. Teach your dog new tricks. Do things to balance your life.

Leave the paddle at home. Self-doubt, self-criticism, and self-punishment can cripple and immobilize even the best of leaders. No one is perfect. We all make mistakes. No leader is blameless or beyond error. We need to accept our faults and weaknesses, as well as our strengths. When you become a leader of a group, don't be too demanding on yourself. Don't beat yourself up after every minor mistake. Be gentler on yourself. Leave the paddle at home.

Leave room to learn. One marvelous way to look at all problems and conflicts with others is to see them as an opportunity to learn a lesson about yourself.

Suppose some jerk tries to push into your lane during a traffic jam. Cars are at a standstill and he aims his front bumper toward your car and creeps in your direction. He doesn't smile at you or even make any eye contact to acknowledge his intentions. He thinks he owns the road. Well, you could pull up to prevent his entry into that tiny space between you and the car in front of you. You could honk and communicate your annoyance. You could yell something really terrible to him. You could even aim your car in his direction and play a little two-mile-per-hour chicken. You could do all kinds of terrible things.

Another way you can look at it is as a lesson to learn something wonderful about yourself. I know this may sound a little corny, but it can work wonders. You can see the situation as an opportunity to learn unselfish, altruistic courtesy and kindness. You can let the jerk (I mean person) into the space in front of you.

This would have been unthinkable to me a few years ago, but since I've been trying to take this new approach to driving and actually let people pull in front of me, I've changed a little. I have learned I'm capable of being kind in a situation when I could be rude and vindictive. I've learned to be courteous and not even expect a brief wave of thanks from the driver. I've learned to let people have the space I once occupied. I've learned to let go a little more. And it's made all the difference in the world.

I've taken an old problem and chosen to see it as a way to learn to be a little kinder to others, without expecting anything in return. This is how you can also choose to view the problems and conflicts you may experience as the leader of a group. During your tenure as leader, people will aim their cars at you, wanting things you may not want to give up. But choose not to see it always as a challenge to fight, or an opportunity to assert your power. See it as an invitation to learn some new things about yourself.

As the group leader, be open to discovering the many untapped skills, characteristics, and talents that still lie hidden from your conscious mind. You are much more complicated, competent, and caring than you think. Be open to discovering more and more about yourself as you lead others.

Any group member can participate in leadership functions—those behaviors that help the group reach its goal. As you assume leadership responsibilities, I hope that you will also assume the attitude of a servant as you create opportunities for your group to be productive and successful. You can encourage the personal growth of your group members as you band together to solve the problems that brought you together.

INDIVIDUAL AND GROUP EXERCISES

8.1 Interview a Leader

Select a leader you have worked with in the past or present who you feel is an effective leader. This individual could be a project manager, a committee chairperson, a supervisor at work, a coach, a personnel director, a scoutmaster, the president of your PTA, and so on. Arrange for a fifteen-minute interview to gather his or her insights concerning leadership. Review the suggestions for interviewing presented in Chapter 6 before you request the interview. Here are some possible questions for your interview:

> What is the single most important lesson you learned from
> leading others?
> What do you like best about leadership?
> What do you like least about leadership?
> What do you do to increase the group's task effectiveness?
> What do you do to increase the group's social effectiveness?
> What specific suggestions can you give for becoming an
> effective leader?

How did your interview go? Did you remember to send a thank-you card? What things did you learn about leadership from your interview?

Are there any suggestions or insights you could incorporate into your leadership skills or knowledge? Did your perceptions or feelings about this individual change after the interview? How? What is the most important lesson you learned from interviewing this individual?

8.2 Leadership Role-Play

With a group of five classmates, work on a simple task (such as planning a group picnic or constructing a midterm exam). Select one group member to role-play an autocratic leader for ten minutes. Then have the same individual role-play a laissez-faire leader during the next ten minutes. For the final ten minutes, have the individual role-play a democratic leader. How did the group members feel about each leadership style? How did the role-player feel about playing the leadership style? What did the group learn about leadership during this exercise?

8.3 Leading a Problem-Analysis Meeting

It's time to put all those neat leadership skills to some practical use. Using the suggestions presented in this chapter, lead a small-group meeting for at least twenty minutes to discuss (not solve) a very small, specific task with four or five people from your work, religious organization, school, or community. If you cannot locate a group outside class, lead a group of four or five classmates to discuss some minor campus problem for twenty minutes. Once you have formed the group, agree on a meeting time and place, construct a five-point agenda to analyze the problem, and review the suggestions for holding an effective meeting presented in this chapter. Lead the group. After the meeting, have group members give you feedback on what they liked and disliked about your meeting. Remember, be a servant leader!

Building a Cohesive Group

We cannot live for only ourselves,
a thousand fibers connect us with our fellow men.

HERMAN MELVILLE

Each weekly quality-control meeting began the same magical way—every group member shared one new or significant thing that had happened since the last meeting. Group members spoke for only twenty seconds as they went around the table to check in, but this brief activity let them touch base with one another—to connect at the human level before conducting regular business.

Occasionally, these check-ins would elevate the group to another level. Once, a woman shared that her high-school daughter's leukemia was in remission. One man revealed that he was afraid to propose to his girlfriend. Another woman proudly announced that she had parachuted from 9,000 feet the previous weekend. These and a hundred other bits of life were experienced collectively during the sixteen months this group met; each sharing brought these people closer together as a team.

After meeting weekly for six months, Barbara, the team leader, missed four consecutive meetings due to a business trip. Doug, a second-level production manager, began the first meeting with a nervously delivered joke, and then proceeded with the agenda. Toward the end of that meeting, Carlos asked Doug if they could check in at the next meeting. The rest of the group quickly agreed.

"I miss hearing what everyone has been up," said JoAnn. "It's one of the few times we get to really connect."

"Plus, it makes me like you guys, which is a miracle." joked Brian.

"I think it makes our meetings much more productive, too," added Vaveck.

At the second meeting, the group spent the first few minutes checking in. Doug began the next two meetings with the check-ins and started to feel a real connection with people who were strangers just weeks before. He also observed a positive difference in his own attitude and behavior during those meetings.

At the fourth meeting's check-in, Doug shared that he believed that the group members' connection at this personal level helped them weather some difficult disagreements. He told them that he appreciated not only how productive the group was, but also how close he had grown to feel about them. Doug admitted that he had never experienced anything like this before and wished he could join them for their remaining eleven months. And he did.

This chapter will examine ways that you can create a caring attitude and build a social dimension within your group to encourage cooperation and productivity. If group members discover some level of personal success, connection, value, support, and trust during the process of working with one another, they will more likely experience a social dimension that produces a cohesive group.

THE SOCIAL DIMENSION

The social dimension of a group lives on long after the task has been completed. Feelings of successful cooperation, connection, appreciation, support, and trust derived from the group experience can play a significant role in shaping and strengthening a member's self-concept. If the social dimension is characterized by competition, apprehension, and mistrust, however, the group experience can impact the individual's self-concept and attitude in a negative way for years to come.

> Work can provide one with a shared smile, a friend for life, and the liberation of the soul.
>
> THOMAS MOORE

The significance of the social dimension cannot be overstated. Without a healthy, supportive social climate in which to conduct the work of the group, task effectiveness can be compromised (Fisher and Ellis, 1990; Shaw, 1981).

Whereas the goal of the group's task dimension is productivity, the goal of the social dimension is **cohesion**—the attraction and connection of group members to one another and to the group.

FEELING SUCCESSFUL

The primary reason for the group's existence is to solve a problem or complete a task. Experiencing success in problem solving or task completion can contribute to building a cohesive group. Members of an athletic team who win all their games during a season will more likely feel connected to one another than will members of a team who lose every game. Successful goal attainment plays a significant role in how members feel about one another and themselves. Without experiencing some level of goal achievement, a group often deteriorates into a collection of frustrated, disconnected, and disappointed individuals.

Here are four steps you can take to bring success to your group—agreeing on the group's goal, formulating minigoals, emphasizing group cooperation, and achieving personal goals.

Agreeing on the Group's Goal

Make certain that each group member agrees on the group's goal. A group cannot be successful in achieving a goal if confusion or disagreement exists about what that goal is. Agreement on the goal can be accomplished during the second step of the problem-solving agenda—analysis of the problem. During this phase, the group formulates the question of policy ("What should be done about . . . ?" or "What should our policy be toward . . . ?"). This step provides the group with its task goal. Without a clearly defined and agreed-upon goal, the group drifts aimlessly.

Formulating Minigoals

You can formulate minigoals—breaking down the larger goal into its smaller or component parts—to make your group experience success more often. For instance, instead of focusing solely on eliminating neighborhood theft, your group may want to break down this larger goal into its incremental parts. Smaller goals can include gathering information from law-enforcement agencies, conducting an attitude survey of neighbors, holding an informational meeting for the neighborhood, and distributing a list of possible solutions to neighbors for their input.

When I chair a group, I construct a list of minigoals with suggested completion dates and the name of the individual responsible for each goal. I distribute this list to group members at the beginning of each meeting, and they announce the progress of their particular minigoal to date. I've found that people enjoy bragging about their minigoal achievement and appreciate the compliments from group members.

Another advantage to formulating minigoals is it divides the labor among the group. No one is stuck doing all the work. When a group member, through choice or circumstance, is left with an inordinate amount of responsibility, the social dimension of the group can suffer. It is more effective from a task point of view to divide the labor and assign minigoals to each member. Most important, it provides each person with added opportunities to experience success during the process of attempting to achieve the larger group goal.

Emphasizing Group Cooperation

To move your group toward success, you can emphasize group cooperation rather than competition. A group that encourages competition among its members will often experience a social dimension characterized by mistrust, selfishness, and rivalry. When members attempt to outdo one another, or to win at the expense of someone else's loss, they threaten the group's cohesiveness. Competition creates a win-lose atmosphere. And where there are losers, there are individuals who don't feel good about themselves.

Here are two ways to emphasize cooperation within your group. First, divide the group into subgroups of two or three individuals and make each subgroup responsible for a minigoal. This will provide members with the opportunity to work together in a smaller group setting, helping to build teamwork and intimacy. Second, hold what I refer to as an "expert session," where some group members share a problem they might be experiencing with their minigoal and other group members try to provide helpful or "expert" information or advice. This also emphasizes cooperation between members.

Achieving Personal Goals

Although the primary function of each group member is to participate and contribute toward the achievement of the group goal, there are also concurrent personal needs each individual hopes to satisfy while participating in the group. Many times these personal needs are minor and incidental, such as the need to investigate a new topic, use a new communication skill, or brag about an interview. Other times, they can serve as the primary motivation or reason for seeking group membership. Loneliness, underappreciation, and a desire for control are some examples of why someone seeks group membership to satisfy personal needs.

You can make it possible to satisfy these needs by having group members state any personal needs they may be conscious of during the orientation phase. After group members introduce themselves, I also have them state one or two personal goals they would like to achieve during the course of our group work.

Most of the time, individuals share personal goals that can be easily achieved during the course of the group's life. I will occasionally use a meeting check-in to give group members an opportunity to share any progress they made toward their personal goals. I devote three to five minutes to the personal goal check-in activity every third meeting. This can do wonders for building a cohesive group.

FEELING CONNECTED

Another way to build a cohesive group is to make each member feel connected to the other members. Some groups are characterized by an atmosphere of distance, coolness, and indifference, whereas other groups enjoy an atmosphere of connection, inclusion, and trust. Here are some ways you can make your group members feel connected and included in the group setting—acknowledging others, structuring an all-channel network, being interested in others, and socializing as a group.

Acknowledging Others

Do not forget to welcome group members as they arrive to the meeting before it begins. Greet them with a smile and use their first names. It's amazing what a smile, a handshake, and a first name will do to make someone feel welcomed and included. If group members are not included in the premeeting chitchat, go over and say hello. Offer them a cup of coffee. Ask how their day went. These simple acts of acknowledging someone's presence can determine the emotional experience for an individual's entire meeting. If in doubt, smile and do your best to make someone feel included and connected to the group. That can be your most important act of the entire meeting.

Structuring an All-Channel Network

Group members may feel more connected when the group process is structured around an all-channel network system. A **communication**

network is the arrangement of communication flow within a system. With an **all-channel network** each group member has access to all other members without having to go through the leader or a central gatekeeper. Each member is free to speak and listen directly to every other group member.

There are a number of things you can do to ensure an all-channel network in your group. First, from a purely physical point of view, have the group always sit in a circle. Arrange the seating into a circle before the meeting begins, and ask latecomers to join the circle upon arrival. A circle configuration permits contact among all members. It discourages members from feeling left out, as might be the case if the group sat in rows or at a long table. Second, have group members exchange phone numbers and e-mail addresses. This enables everyone to have access to other group members and contact them directly. Third, discourage dialogue between two individuals during a group discussion. Whenever two members begin to conduct an extended conversation, interrupt them and bring the discussion back to the group. Often, two powerful group members will dominate discussion, reducing the process to a dialogue rather than a group communication. Don't permit this to occur. For a cohesive group, provide open and equal access to communication.

Being Interested in Others

Our lives are busy and we often find ourselves with little time to become acquainted even with those we work with. Feeling connected to others can also be achieved by taking a moment or two to show an interest in another group member.

Rather than seeing others as merely cogs in the machinery, you can devote a brief period of time before and after each meeting to initiate a more personal discussion with another group member. Avoid getting into anything too deep and heavy, but you can show an interest in another person by simply asking questions about family, hobbies, sports, interests, and so on. Don't force anything. Be gentle and friendly. Remember, the point is to connect with another person. The actual content of your after-meeting conversation is not nearly as important as your showing interest in another person by asking questions and listening attentively.

> Practice being interested in others.
>
> WILLIAM FORESTER

Socializing as a Group

Some of the most famous electronic companies in the world owe a large part of their accomplishments to their legendary Friday gatherings. Companies like Apple Computer, Tandem, National Semiconductor, and Rolm are famous for their socializing on Friday afternoons. Over food, drink, and music, employees from every level of the corporation get together informally to talk shop and socialize. These companies have discovered that the Friday gatherings are a wonderfully enjoyable way to have fun, become better acquainted, and solve work-related problems.

You may want to do something along these lines with your own group. It's not necessary to throw a $5,000 bash on a Friday afternoon for the six members of your group, but you may offer to treat the group to pizza and soft drinks after the next meeting or bring refreshments to the meeting. Offer your home for a potluck dinner the next time your group is scheduled to meet.

Whatever you try, look for ways to occasionally socialize with your group, after or even during the meeting. When we socialize, we change our demeanor and the group has a new frame of reference from which to work. Socializing with group members is one of the most enjoyable and powerful ways to enhance the social dimension of any collection of people.

FEELING VALUED

In addition to needing to experience task success and feel connected to the group, members need to feel valued for their effort and contributions. Expressions of appreciation and compliments contribute to a strong social dimension in any group, and serve an especially vital function in building a cohesive group. When group members feel valued for their effort, their loyalty and commitment to the group are strengthened. You can make people feel valued in your group by seeing the best in others, communicating appreciation, and sharing compliments.

Seeing the Best in Others

When was the last time you told someone you appreciated them? Have you communicated appreciation to someone in the last day? How about the past week? We are often so busy, so preoccupied, and so involved with our own lives, we neglect to notice and appreciate others. In your group, you need to become more appreciative by seeing the best in others and communicating your appreciation of them.

I have a theory about life: On any given day, 80 percent of our life is working well and only 20 percent of our life is not working at an acceptable level. I call it my 80/20 rule.

Roughly 80 percent of your work life, your personal relationships, your body, your automobile, your yard tools, and so on are working or performing at an acceptable level. The other 20 percent is not. Yet when you stop and think about it, we often give that 20 percent of our lives 100 percent of our attention. We become fixated on a critical remark from our boss. We obsess about someone else getting a raise. We worry about an overdrawn check. We spend a great deal of time and effort fretting about 20 percent of those things that aren't going well, while we ignore the 80 percent of our lives that is functioning well.

The 80/20 rule also operates in groups. We often tend to focus our attention on the 20 percent of frustrations, disappointments, and failures experienced by the group, and neglect the 80 percent that is successful.

In order to appreciate others, we need to wear new glasses. We need to look for those things, both big and little, that are working. We need to notice that everyone arrived at the meeting on time. We need to see that everyone contributed something to the discussion. We need to recognize that we made some progress on reaching consensus. We need to be aware of the subtle attempts of some members to improve how they interact during discussion. We need to see the best, not the worst, of what is happening in this moment.

Communicating Appreciation

Once you've decided to see the best in every situation—to concentrate on the 80 percent of the group process that is working well—you need to verbally communicate your appreciation. Simply make an I-statement of appreciation: "Yung, I appreciated your efforts in having us reach consensus this morning," "Alison, I appreciated the questions you asked that helped me clarify my thoughts during the meeting," and "Victor, I thank you for letting me put my report on the agenda today."

These aren't long, involved statements, just short messages of appreciation and thanks. They take only a moment or two of your time, but can remain with the recipient for a lifetime. Try to communicate the appreciation you feel inside. It will be worth your effort.

Sharing Compliments

Everyone appreciates a compliment. During the course of your group work, you can compliment someone's effort, achievement, and character.

Complimenting effort. One area we neglect to compliment others on is effort. We usually reserve our compliments for those moments when the first-place trophy is awarded, when the final problem is solved, or when the last obstacle is overcome. But those moments are few and far between. We need to notice and compliment the effort our fellow group members are putting forth right now, long before any problem is solved or any trophies are awarded. A simple statement complimenting members' efforts can really encourage those who may feel their efforts are going unnoticed. Compliment a person's efforts and you'll take another step toward building a cohesive group. You may make friends, too!

Complimenting achievement. Whenever a group member achieves some task or personal goal, verbally compliment the individual in front of the group (and personally after the meeting). Public complimenting of task or personal achievements builds solidarity and goodwill within the group. It communicates an unselfish, appreciative attitude on your part, and models complimentary behavior to other group members. Remember, your own behavior can have a ripple effect on the entire group. Compliment the achievements of others. It's amazing how productive a group can be when its members applaud the achievements of one another.

Complimenting character. Who a person is, not what he or she has achieved, can be the focus of your compliment. Honesty, integrity, patience, understanding, caring, kindness, compassion, and humor are just some character components you may want to compliment.

Rarely are individuals complimented on their character strengths. They might not even be aware of a particular facet of their character until you bring it to their attention. Complimenting character publicly in the group can also serve to draw attention and focus to a certain kind of behavior or attitude you want reinforced within the group. Show your appreciation for them by complimenting their character.

FEELING SUPPORTED

Making the members feel supported helps to build a cohesive group. Often during our lives we may feel no one understands us, no one cares, and no one is there to lend a helping hand. I think we've all felt this way a time or two. Whether it's showing understanding for someone who is frustrated with a group task or experiencing the pain of a recent divorce, acts of support can deepen the social dimension of a group. A group can do a great deal to provide support for its members by communicating empathy, communicating caring, and giving assistance.

Communicating Empathy

Empathy is the ability to take the perspective of the other and feel what the other is experiencing. This doesn't mean you need to assist, correct, or rescue the other person. It means you can understand or feel what the other person is feeling. An empathic response is often the only thing an individual wants—to feel that someone understands. No desire for evaluation, advice, or even assistance; just someone who understands.

Earlier we discussed listening for the speaker's feelings and ways to reflect those feelings back to the speaker. This is the primary way you can demonstrate empathy—to mirror feelings.

If you feel group members could use the support that empathy provides, try listening for their emotional messages. Listen to how they may be feeling. Then reflect those feelings with active listening: "Sounds like you're really frustrated about . . . ," "You're feeling upset about . . . ," or "Sounds as if you're really happy about . . ."

Merely reflecting what you think the speaker is feeling and experiencing is a powerful way to demonstrate empathy. Notice that some of the statements dealt with positive feelings also. Empathy involves both positive and negative feelings. So be open and sensitive to reflecting both. Let them feel understood.

Communicating Caring

You can communicate your support to a group member by telling them so. Once you understand what an individual is experiencing and you have demonstrated empathy, you can go the next step and communicate your concern. Nothing heavy. Just a word or two expressing concern or caring. Statements of caring and support can be very encouraging and uplifting. Here are some ways to communicate this form of support: "I hope things work out for you . . . ," "I know you'll be fine . . . ," and "I support your decision to . . ."

When fellow group members suffer frustration with a task, experience conflict with another member, or fall behind on their group assignment, a word of encouragement or concern can make a difference in their attitude and resolve. We all need to know others care about what is going on with us. A brief sentence or two communicating caring can raise the spirits of a disappointed or discouraged individual.

Giving Assistance

In addition to demonstrating empathy and communicating caring, you should offer your assistance to other group members if you have an inclination to help and are in a position to do so. Most of the time such assistance will include making a copy of a report, helping with the overhead projector, or distributing written material. Sometimes your assistance might require more involvement, such as constructing a visual aid, typing a report, or giving a ride to the airport.

Take the opportunity to lend a helping hand. I know you have a million things to do yourself, but you can be of tremendous support to another member and will nurture a cooperative spirit within the group. Don't be selfish with your time and energy if you see an opportunity to lend some help. The recipient of your help will remember your gesture, and the relationship between the two of you will change for the better.

Someone once said, "The purpose of life is to help others make it through." You can make the group experience truly meaningful and significant if you help others. Your willingness to put your caring into action will do more to improve cohesion and commitment toward one another than any other act I know. It proves your support.

TRUSTING OTHERS

Although people may feel included, acknowledged, valued, and supported in a group, the experience can be diluted and even negated if they sense an intentional manipulation or deception.

A furniture salesperson can make us feel acknowledged and included. In fact, she can compliment, praise, and flatter us with expert mastery, but deep down we realize this is her job. She wants to manipulate and control us, to sell us, to get something from us. But in the end, do we really believe her compliments, warmth, and friendliness? Most likely not.

For the social dimension of a group to achieve true cohesiveness, group members must trust one another. They need to trust that what

> The only way to make a person trustworthy is to trust him.
>
> HENRY STIMSON

others are saying is honest and true. They need to trust that others' support and assistance are sincere. They need to trust that others' warmth and friendship are genuine and heartfelt. Without this trust, all the other components necessary to building a cohesive group are suspect.

What indicators of trustworthiness are there? What clues can we search for in determining the level of trust we can give a particular individual? How do we know we can believe what someone is telling us?

The answer is we can't. No one can measure or predict with complete accuracy the truthfulness of another individual's statement or behavior. There are no fail-proof tests, no totally accurate examinations. The best we can do is to assign probabilities to another person's honesty based on our past experiences with this individual. Oftentimes we are 99.99 percent certain that a person's statements are true or his behavior is sincerely motivated. But we are occasionally shocked by that 0.01 percent of the time when our predictions are wrong, and a trusted friend, colleague, or acquaintance lies or behaves in a dishonest way.

For group members to experience a high degree of cohesiveness, they must have a certain level of trust in one another—a basic trust that what an individual member says is true. That behavior accurately portrays the member's internal feelings and intentions. Without this trust, there can be no extended cooperation within the group, because communication would be doubted and behavior would be suspect.

Although there are no fail-proof tests for trusting others, there are two things you can ask to improve your decision to trust a certain individual. Does that person keep his or her word? How does that person treat others?

Does That Person Keep His or Her Word?

Does an individual arrive at meetings on time? Can that person keep a promise to show up on time or even show up at all? Does the person complete assigned tasks or make up excuses or blame others for failure to finish a job? When someone makes you a promise to do something, does that person actually follow through and make good on the promise? After a time, do you continue to believe or do you disregard the person's commitments to you?

If certain individuals keep their word, you should be more likely to believe what they say is true. This doesn't work all the time. There are exceptions to every rule. But a person who keeps promises is a better risk, as far as trusting is concerned, than someone who does not keep promises. Who keeps promises in your group?

How Does That Person Treat Others?

An individual's conduct with others is important to observe when determining whether to trust or distrust someone. How does this individual treat others? Does this person gossip about others when the target of the gossip is absent? Does this person lie or exaggerate the truth when communicating with others? Do you sense manipulation or calculation in the person's actions and dealings with others? Is this person inordinately complimentary or flattering to others in the group? In general, do you trust the way the person treats others?

These two methods for determining the trustworthiness of an individual are helpful, but in the end, you must decide for yourself. For the purposes of decision making and problem solving in small groups, I assume the best and trust each group member to participate in an open, honest, and responsible manner. From this frame of reference, I can begin the group experience positively and optimistically.

GROUPTHINK: WHEN GROUPS ARE TOO COHESIVE

Making group members feel successful, included, acknowledged, supported, and trusted are five ingredients that make group members feel committed and dedicated to one another. The social climate of the group will determine its task effectiveness. It is the social dimension experience that lives on in the memories and hearts of group members long after the task has been completed.

But you need to be careful that your group does not become *too* cohesive. The primary threat to sound decision making and problem solving with a group that experiences extreme cohesiveness is a phenomenon called **groupthink**.

Sociologist Irving Janis coined the term "groupthink" to describe the situation when a group departs from rational, reality-based decision making to irrational, nonreality-based decision making, because they are too cohesive. Although groupthink doesn't manifest itself very often in groups at work or school, it is important to understand the factors that move a group to think it can do no wrong.

You can recognize groupthink when a group believes it is invulnerable and no harm can come to it. This perception is not based in reality, but is due to the extreme cohesiveness of the group. Once the group perceives itself as invulnerable, its decisions can involve more risk than the group would normally accept. The second way to recognize groupthink is by observing unusual pressure toward conformity. Dissent is discouraged and the group moves toward the majority view. Even if their ideas and proposals appear extreme to the group members themselves, they feel morally justified to pursue their objectives. Closed-mindedness is the final way you can recognize groupthink. The group will rationalize its decisions, even when the evidence points to contrary conclusions or a group member raises objections to the group's course of action.

It's important for you to be aware of these signs of groupthink and occasionally measure the behavior of your group against them. Does your group think no harm can come to it? Does it pressure its members toward conformity? Is it closed-minded?

If you answered yes to any of these questions, you need to consider the extent to which they are true. Simply because a group is occasionally closed-minded does not necessarily mean it is experiencing groupthink. But if your group experiences some of these telltale signs for an extended period of time, you would be wise to bring them to the group's attention.

The best way to avoid groupthink is to take precautionary steps. It's much better to avoid the development of groupthink from the beginning than attempt to eliminate it once it's established. Here are four ways to prevent groupthink from developing in your group:

1. **The leader should stress critical evaluation.** From the very first meeting, the group leader should emphasize the role each group member is required to play in critically evaluating and analyzing the decision-making process of the group.
2. **Seek outside feedback.** Each group member should discuss the decision-making processes with trusted colleagues outside the group and report these "outside" perceptions to the group.

3. **Assign a devil's advocate within the group.** The leader can assign one group member to play the role of devil's advocate to challenge the prevailing ideas and proposals of the majority. The role of devil's advocate should be given to a different group member for each meeting.
4. **Invite outside observation.** The group can occasionally invite a qualified individual from outside to observe the decision-making process of the group.

Use these techniques to keep the decision-making process in your group open, subject to critical analysis, and reality-based. Everything you do in your group affects each member in some way. A smile, a compliment, or an invitation for coffee can change a life. You may never fully realize your impact on the group members, but I encourage you to discover the caring, sensitive, and loving aspects of who you are. Perhaps it will be in a group that you discover many beautiful things about yourself.

Remember that each group member has personal needs and desires that transcend the goals and needs of the group. Rather than deny or ignore this personal dimension of each group member, you can implement many of the suggestions outlined in this chapter to create a sensitive, caring, and cohesive group. Group cohesiveness will enhance the group's ability to complete the tasks before it.

INDIVIDUAL AND GROUP EXERCISES

9.1 Sharing Appreciation

Reflect on your personal life and notice the 80 percent that is working well. From the list of things in your life that are going smoothly, select one individual who is currently contributing to this process. Perhaps it's a friend who occasionally calls just to see how you're doing. Maybe it's a coworker who gave you a hand on a project the other day. Possibly your roommate was especially thoughtful or concerned this morning. Thank that person with some home-baked cookies, a bouquet of flowers from your backyard, a gift certificate to your favorite restaurant, or some other token of your appreciation. Let this person know you value his or her role in your life.

9.2 **Personal Goals for New Groups**

When the members of a group meet for the first time and chart out their initial plans and agendas for the work that lies ahead, they often neglect the social dimension of the group. They will fail to consider and become aware of the personal needs and goals of the group members. A new group can use this exercise to encourage the group's social dimension.

Meet with five classmates who have never before worked together in a group. During your first meeting, share one personal goal you would like to accomplish during your time with the group. Goals such as improving listening, being more punctual, handling conflict more constructively, receiving criticism, being more caring, and becoming more assertive are common aspirations. Invite the other members to also describe a personal goal they would like to achieve. If each group member shares one goal, the awareness of all the group members will be greatly increased in terms of knowing what people are trying to accomplish. Then move onto the main task.

During the course of meetings, the group should devote a few minutes at the beginning or end of each discussion to review members' individual progress on their personal goals and receive the kind of acknowledgment, encouragement, and thanks they desire. Give this a try. It will help you create a caring, sensitive group.

After several meetings, discuss how this process is working for each member. Do the individuals feel more connected? How is this enhanced social dimension affecting the group's task dimension?

9.3 **Devil's Advocate in the Group**

Meet with a group of four or five classmates and attempt to solve a miniproblem. Once the group begins to reach consensus on a proposed solution, have one member play the role of devil's advocate. The role-player should question the reasoning and opinions of the majority membership. The devil's advocate should raise objections to the proposed solution and continue to object for at least ten minutes.

How did the devil's advocate influence the group? How did the role-player feel? How did the other members feel? What positive contributions can a devil's advocate make to the group process?

CHAPTER TEN

Managing Conflict

The art of living lies less in eliminating conflicts than in growing with them.

BERNARD BARUCH

The refrigerator light cast a white glow on the two young boys as they sat on the kitchen floor, bickering with each other. Between the two brothers was a plate containing the last slice of apple pie, which they were going to share. Holding the butter knife in one hand, the seven-year-old was trying to cut the piece in two, while the younger brother was grabbing at the knife, complaining he always got the smaller piece when his brother was in charge of dividing the remains of a dessert. Back and forth they bickered as they tugged on the butter knife. Then their mom entered the scene of the conflict.

"What are you kids fighting about now?" asked the mother.

"When Tyler cuts the pie, he always gives me the smallest piece," complained the younger brother.

"I do not," Tyler shot back.

"You do too," yelled Jared.

"Do not."

"Do too."

"Okay, you guys. Settle down. I've got an idea," suggested the mom. "How about one of you cuts the pie and the other gets to select the first piece."

Smiles slowly broke out on both the young boys' faces.

"All right, I'll still cut the pie," said Tyler. And he did. But Tyler never measured, eyed, and remeasured a piece of pie so carefully as he did this one, because he knew Jared got to choose. So he cut the piece perfectly in half.

Jared eyed both pieces carefully and selected the one he wanted, but Tyler didn't mind because each piece was exactly the same size. Both parties agreed to a solution they found acceptable. The conflict was peacefully resolved, but it wouldn't be the last before they went to sleep.

"And shut that refrigerator door!" the mom said as she winked at the boys.

This chapter will present three step-by-step processes designed to resolve procedural, interpersonal, and substantive conflict within a group. You will also learn a variety of specific interventions you can use for each of the five dysfunctional communication styles that might arise in your group work with others. By using these approaches to resolve differences, you can create an atmosphere where conflict can be dealt with in a healthy, productive fashion.

A Different Approach to Conflict

The mother in the opening story could have settled the conflict in many ways. She could have ignored the battle and walked past the skirmish. She could have punished both boys for fighting. She could have eaten the pie herself to teach the boys a lesson.

But she didn't. She flowed with their conflict. She joined their little clash and suggested an alternative that required their cooperation and produced an acceptable solution they were both happy with. If only the rest of our conflicts could be so easily resolved.

In your small-group work, you and the other members will occasionally experience conflict: a struggle over the placement of an item on the agenda, an argument over the merits of a proposed solution, a disagreement between two group members. These and other situations can reduce the group's task effectiveness and strain the relationships of its members.

> The resistance to the unpleasant situation is the root of suffering.
>
> RAM DASS

Group members can ignore or deny conflict. They can address it indirectly through innuendo and insinuation. They can be more direct and blame and punish. They can even expel the member causing conflict. They, like the mother of the two boys, have many methods at their disposal for dealing with conflict.

Small groups often employ counterproductive approaches in dealing with conflict. They close their eyes. They blame. They hit. They hurt. Yet such approaches do very little to resolve conflict. In many instances they serve to escalate differences, increase tension, and sever relationships within the group.

An old Zen saying suggests another approach to dealing with conflict: "Hug your problem and it may disappear." This may sound paradoxical. Hug your problem? Aren't we trained to run from conflict? Don't we at least find someone to blame for the mess to distance us from responsibility? "It's not my fault," we say. I think the "hugging" suggestion is actually an invitation to get closer to conflict rather than further away. It suggests a direct and open exploration of conflict, without blame or punishment. Conflict can be a wonderful teacher. It can teach us valuable lessons about others and ourselves. Instead of always trying to ignore, deny, blame, or fight during conflict, we can choose to join it. Acknowledge its presence openly. Explore rather than blame. Loosen rather than tighten. We need to flow with our conflict.

MYTHS OF CONFLICT

Conflict is a struggle or disagreement between two or more options or people. This struggle or disagreement can be over differences of opinions, beliefs, or values in the task dimension of the group. Conflict can also be experienced in the social dimension between two or more people having differences in feelings, perceptions, and behaviors. Three commonly held myths concerning conflict are that conflict should be avoided at all costs, conflict is always someone else's fault, and all conflict can be resolved.

Myth 1: Avoid Conflict at All Costs

One of the most common ways to deal with conflict is to avoid it. Now, this is good advice if you're walking down a dark alley and you see three figures lurking behind the garbage bins. You should turn and walk the other way. Sometimes conflict, or possible conflict, can and should be avoided.

But in your small-group efforts, don't avoid conflict at all costs. Conflict can often benefit the task and social dimensions of the group. In fact, conflict can be an opportunity to listen to differences, discover new common ground, and uncover more effective ways to interact together as a group. It's out of the differences of group members that strength is built and wiser decisions are made.

Myth 2: Conflict Is Always Someone Else's Fault

Frequently, our first response when conflict occurs is to find someone to blame. It's what I call the "blame first, explore later" syndrome. We find fault, and then we may examine what the problem really was. Many times we fail to explore the various factors of a disagreement or dispute. We want to blame. Maybe because we can't be at fault if someone else is to blame. In the complexity of group work, there may not be someone at fault or someone to blame. Maybe we're barking up the wrong tree when we automatically look for a culprit rather than examine the disagreement at hand. Anytime five or six people work together, there will be, and should be, differences of opinion. When these differences surface, instead of finding someone to blame or fault, explore and examine. Your group will function better when you do.

Myth 3: All Conflict Can Be Resolved

The final myth is that all conflict can be resolved. The belief is that if we try hard enough, if we talk long enough, and if we compromise well enough, we will eventually resolve whatever conflict is before us. This is not always the case.

Not all substantive or idea conflicts can be resolved in a manner acceptable to all parties. Especially those issues concerning questions of value. Conflicts centered on what is morally, ethically, and theologically correct and true may never be satisfactorily resolved in the group. Deep-seated personality conflicts between two group members may never be adequately resolved and healed during the life of the group.

Some conflicts may never be resolved. That's okay. That's life. Not every relationship works. Not every dream is realized. Not every desire gets satisfied. The lesson can be to learn to let go in situations like this, give in to another individual's wishes, accommodate others for the sake of the group. Not all conflict can be resolved. It may ultimately involve our departure from the group.

ADVANTAGES OF CONFLICT

Anytime conflict exists within a group, there is always the potential for growth for each group member. This growth can take the form of expanded awareness, improved participation, increased productivity, greater cohesiveness, and developed maturity.

Expanded Awareness

Many times when a group is running smoothly, its members working together cooperatively, there is a sense of satisfaction, a feeling of well-being. Complacency can result. A deadening of the senses can occur, which may cause a trancelike state. If you've ever ridden on a train across flat land for an extended time, you know how quickly the monotony of the ride can lull you to sleep.

When conflict is brought out into the open, it can have an arousing effect upon group members. They are awakened from the productive hum of their routines. They are called to process, interact, and behave in a different, more focused manner. They are now in the midst of a conflict! The shift in focus from the mundane to the exceptional can be stimulating. It can wake us from our sleep.

Improved Participation

Just as the mere introduction of open conflict to the group process can foster expanded awareness, it can also encourage increased participation from group members. Many times, members will spring to action and participate with greater frequency and enthusiasm when the discussion turns to matters of dispute and struggle. In fact, many a relationship has been based upon this one variable—conflict.

Increased Productivity

The results of disagreement over substantive and procedural conflicts can benefit the productivity of the group. When the group resolves conflict and discovers new solutions, ideas, and procedures, the productivity can be greater than before the conflict. The labor pains brought about by conflict may also signal the birth of fresh ideas, better solutions, and improved relationships.

Greater Cohesiveness

After the group deals with conflict in a productive and healthy manner, the group's cohesiveness can be greatly enhanced. A better understanding and working relationship often result from conflicts between group members if the group handles the conflict positively and maturely. Once group members share perceptions, air differences, and establish new common ground for interacting and relating to one another, they can share more intimate feelings of connection.

Cohesion within the group frequently occurs also when the group resolves substantive conflicts regarding the task dimension. With the struggle over a specific task successfully negotiated and put behind them, the group can experience a feeling of achievement and intimacy. Good work often fosters good feelings.

Developed Maturity

Conflict within a group can help an individual increase in maturity. By that I mean, grow up. Each one of us is childish and infantile in certain areas of our lives. Having to butt heads and hearts with other human beings in our group can provide us with a rich growing environment in which we can develop our abilities to disengage our egos, practice empathy, exercise patience, respond nondefensively, demonstrate compromise, and ask for forgiveness. These and many other activities brought about by conflict can tremendously benefit our personal growth and development.

TYPES OF GROUP CONFLICT

When you consider the enormous potential for conflict within any group, it's amazing any collection of individuals can work together in relative harmony and reach agreement on any matter. Literally thousands upon thousands of minor and major task and social dimension issues can ignite disagreement and struggle.

Every group experiences conflicts. Each conflict centers on a different issue. The focus is on dissimilarities, yet to address the conflict successfully requires distinctly unique perceptions, approaches, and interventions on the part of group members. No matter what conflict you face, it will fall into one of three categories: procedural, substantive, or interpersonal.

Procedural Conflict (Structure)

A **procedural conflict** deals with the structure or procedures the group follows during discussion. These procedures outline how the meeting will be run, the order of the agenda, how disagreement will be handled, and how decisions will be made. A procedural conflict involves disagreement or struggle over the mechanics of the group's operation.

Substantive Conflict (Issues)

A **substantive conflict** involves disagreement or struggle over the substance or issues of discussion. This type of conflict centers on the task dimension of the group. Substantive conflict can involve disagreement or arguments over the tests of evidence, the analysis of reasoning, the debate over proposed solutions, or any matter that deals with the content of discussion. Whereas a procedural conflict debates the mechanics of how something will be done or conducted within the group, a substantive conflict struggles with the ideas, opinions, beliefs, and values of group members themselves.

Interpersonal Conflict (People)

Tension or conflict between individual members of the group is called **interpersonal conflict** because it involves the feelings and behaviors of individuals. Although interpersonal conflict can often present itself as a procedural or substantive conflict initially, stronger feelings and statements attacking the person (an ad hominem attack) can result, unmasking conflict between people.

Now that you know the basic differences between procedural, substantive, and interpersonal conflicts, I'll present some specific ways to deal with each category.

DEALING WITH PROCEDURAL CONFLICT

Any conflict or struggle aimed at the process or method by which the group works is a procedural conflict. These types of conflicts often involve:

- Changes in the frequency, times, and locations of meetings
- Changes in the agenda format or meeting structure
- Extending or ending debate on a controversial issue
- Modification of decision-making procedures
- Modification of speaking rights/time limits

How to Resolve Procedural Conflict

The group leader or chairperson needs to identify these conflicts, bring them to the group's attention, and act on them. Usually, the leader will have the power to accept or reject a proposed change in the procedures of the group. And the leader's decision is final.

But if there is no designated leader, or the leader wants to employ a more democratic method for discussing and structuring the procedures of the group, the group can adopt a more open process. This process involves the basic parliamentary procedure steps:

1. Have a proposal (motion) stated to the group.
2. Ask if there is a second (a second member supporting the motion).
3. If there isn't a second, the proposal is rejected.
4. If there is a second, the group discusses the proposal.
5. A vote is taken when the discussion is completed.
6. The proposal is either accepted or rejected based on the vote.

I prefer this method when faced with a procedural conflict because it directs the question back to group members, it opens discussion to all, and the decision is based on the majority vote. If the majority of the group votes to accept or reject the proposal, there is usually majority support to enforce the old or new procedure.

DEALING WITH SUBSTANTIVE CONFLICT

The second category of conflict experienced in groups involves ideas and issues. The focus of substantive conflict is *what* the group is discussing, not *how* it is being discussed. These content issues can include disagreement concerning the:

- Reliability of information or evidence
- Reasoning supporting a proposal or idea
- Acceptability of an opinion or idea
- Acceptability of a specific proposal
- Acceptability of a goal or objective of the group

When a group experiences substantive conflict, the leader or the group may attempt to resolve the conflict by avoiding it. The group can drop the issue and move to another topic. The leader can force a decision upon group members, thus eliminating the substantive debate. The leader or group can also try to please members of both sides by using compromise and having both sides give a little ground. Finally, the group can vote to determine which idea will prevail. Each strategy for dealing with substantive conflict reduces the group's effectiveness by prematurely eliminating open and honest discussion of the issue, forcing compromise, and imposing a win-lose atmosphere on the group's social dimension.

How to Resolve Substantive Conflict

An open discussion of the issue is required with all substantive conflict. Whether group members vigorously debate the admissibility of evidence to the discussion and the reasoning of a proposal, or modify the primary purpose of the group, these steps will contribute to a more positive, productive, and successful approach to substantive conflict:

1. **Identify the conflict.** State the substantive conflict in specific terms. Summarize the differences of opinion or sides to the debate.
2. **Share perceptions.** Once you've brought the conflict out for discussion, ask other members for their perceptions of the conflict and the seriousness of the conflict.
3. **Share opinions.** Ask group members to voice their opinions about the issue, but refrain from verbally attacking members with the opposing viewpoint. Remind the group that it is possible to disagree with other people without having to dislike them. Focus on issues, not personalities.
4. **Listen actively.** Whenever an individual has made a statement, have the opposition restate the idea or feeling to the speaker's satisfaction. This listening for understanding will promote more accurate communication and prevent emotions from escalating during discussion.
5. **State the opposition's strengths.** Have the opposing sides point out the strengths in the other's arguments or opinions. This is the difficult one. They usually won't want to state the other's strengths, but if you can get them to participate in this step, you've come a long way to bringing about agreement.
6. **Discover common ground.** Try to have the opposing sides discover something they can both agree on. It doesn't necessarily have to be a major point—just some common ground. Perhaps both sides can agree only that a conflict exists and they will work to resolve the conflict. That's a beginning. From common ground, the two sides can work to discover more points of agreement as the discussion continues.

7. **Take a break.** After heated and often draining debate, a break is in order for the group. Take a five- or ten-minute break to stretch the legs, talk about something else, and get a drink.

8. **Continue the discussion or move on.** After the break, repeat steps 3 to 6 until the sides reach a consensus on how they see the issue, proposal, or group goal. After extended discussion, the group may feel that no common ground or consensus can be reached and will need to discuss how to move on despite difference of opinion. Remind the group of all the things that are working and going well, and that this particular issue is just one of many the group will face in its life.

You might recognize this eight-step process as a modification of the consensus decision-making technique presented in Chapter 5. It should be, because the purpose of consensus is to discover a proposal, decision, or solution to some problem (or conflict) that is workable and acceptable to all group members.

In your dealings with substantive conflicts, keep in mind that the reason people work in small groups is to utilize the best each member is willing and able to contribute to achieve the group's goal. Differences of ideas will inevitably surface, but those differences also constitute the strength of the discussion process. It's the discarding of those ideas the group decides are unnecessary and the retaining of those ideas it feels are valuable that make the group's product superior to the best individual's product.

> To every disadvantage there is a corresponding advantage.
> W. CLEMENT STONE

DEALING WITH INTERPERSONAL CONFLICT

Sometimes there may be conflict between two group members. The interpersonal conflict can be minor and fleeting. Examples of this are inappropriate remarks directed at an individual or a rude comment spoken in frustration, where in each instance, someone was upset or hurt by the comment. The interpersonal conflict can also be major and sustained, as in the case of aggressive and open feuding between two or more group members. Here are some causes of interpersonal conflict:

- Residual emotional injury from substantive or procedural conflict
- Different values and beliefs
- Cultural or racial differences
- Different personalities
- Different communication styles (dysfunctional roles)

No matter what causes the interpersonal conflict, it negatively affects the social dimension of the group because two or more group members experience conflict at the personal level.

Often interpersonal conflict can be disguised as a procedural or substantive conflict, but the real cause of the dispute is a concealed interpersonal conflict between members. Even during legitimate procedural or substantive conflicts, tempers may flare and feelings may get hurt, which can invite retaliation and attack at the personal level. It is often difficult to prevent sustained substantive conflict from developing into interpersonal conflict. Our hearts are connected to our heads in ways we don't yet fully understand.

How to Resolve Interpersonal Conflict Caused by Normal Differences

Most of your interpersonal conflict in the group can be dealt with using the steps suggested here:

1. **Self-check-in.** Before you do anything, just sit and breathe. Don't say anything to the individual you're experiencing difficulty with. Just sit and breathe for now. After the meeting, go home and conduct a five-minute check-in with yourself about this conflict. Ask yourself:

   > What specifically did this person say or do to upset me? Did I overreact? Am I overly sensitive today? How am I doing in other aspects of my life? Am I still upset about what this person said or did?

   Before you do anything, sleep on it. Do you feel the same after you awaken? If you are feeling better, good. Give the individual another chance. If not, go to step 2.

2. **Ask for third-person perception check.** Discuss this matter with another group member who is not involved in the conflict. Briefly share your basic perceptions of the conflict, and then ask this third party for perceptions of the remark, behavior, or event. Did that person share your perceptions? If not, consider the

feedback and put the matter on hold. If the conflict recurs, then start over at step 1. If the third party confirms your perceptions, go to step 3.

3. **Decide what you want.** Next you must determine what you want to do. Do you want to let the incident go? Do you want to share your perceptions with the individual? Do you want to retaliate in kind? Do you want to punish the person? Do you want an apology? What do you really want? Think long and hard about this one. Most of the time, if the conflict was a brief, one-time event (a remark, a joke, an accusation, a slur), you'll let it go and see if it happens again. If you won't let it go, don't consider retaliation, punishment, or even getting an apology. Go to step 4.

4. **Conduct perception check-in with the individual.** After the next meeting, ask the individual if you can meet for a few minutes. If the person asks what you want to discuss, explain that you want to share your perceptions of a recent event involving her. If she refuses, let it go. Then go back to step 1. Don't push the matter. If you can meet, ask for her perceptions of the event. In most instances, the individual will defend the behavior, back off and modify her position, or apologize. If she apologizes, accept the apology, shake hands, and let go of it. If the person backs off and modifies her position, support that position in whatever way you're comfortable and go to step 5. If the person attacks you, disagrees with your perception, or defends her position, remain calm and breathe. Then go to step 5.

5. **State your boundary.** A boundary is an imaginary line that separates what is acceptable to you from what is *not* acceptable to you. If the individual disagreed with your perception, or defended or modified her position, state your boundary about future behavior. A boundary statement is informational, not blaming, accusing, or punishing. Its basic structure is:

> If you _____, then I am prepared to _____.
> If you continue to criticize me in front of the group,
>   then I am prepared to leave the room.
> If you don't bring the video camera to our meeting,
>   then I am prepared to purchase one for the group
>   and bill it to your department.

6. **Enforce your boundary statement.** The very next time the individual repeats the unacceptable behavior, enforce your boundary response. Whether that means identifying the interaction, leaving the meeting room, or bringing the matter to the attention of the group, implement your boundary statement immediately.

This six-step interpersonal conflict resolution model is just that, a model. It provides one way to manage interpersonal conflict. There are other methods you may want to learn about in the future, but this approach is simple and direct. Regardless of your strategy, however, remember that a gentle, open, and sincere attitude on your part will help create an atmosphere in which you can invite the other into dialogue.

SPECIFIC INTERVENTIONS FOR DYSFUNCTIONAL BEHAVIOR

In addition to the six-step interpersonal conflict resolution process, specific interventions for dysfunctional behaviors of group members in any one of the three areas of conflict are helpful to know. A **dysfunctional behavior** is any habitual behavior that disrupts the task and/or social functioning of the group.

Generally, you cannot deal effectively with dysfunctional behaviors using the harmonizing behaviors discussed in Chapter 7. The causes of dysfunctional behavior are more deeply ingrained and beyond the scope of this book. Yet you can try to bring the behavior to the attention of the individual or use some interventions that can help correct the dysfunctional behavior. Here are some interventions to try when you discover mild forms of dysfunctional communication behavior in your group.

Controller Interventions

Controllers try to dominate the discussion by speaking at length, interrupting others, and repeatedly bringing the discussion back to their point of view. Their nonverbal posture is often rigid, tight, and stern. If you notice a member displaying this type of behavior, you can:

Summarize what the controller has said.
State your own opinion when the controller pauses for breath.

> Ask the other group members for their input or feedback.
> Respond to his interrupting by saying, "Were you aware I
>   was speaking?"

If controllers react in a hostile fashion to this type of intervention or continue to exhibit controlling behavior, confront them directly. Don't call controllers names or blame them directly. Your best strategy is to confront controllers personally, away from the group, and share your perceptions of their behavior. Ask for their feedback on your perceptions to initiate a dialogue so that you can (1) request that they give more speaking time to the other group members and (2) actively listen to them. Controllers will not readily give up their attempts at control, however. Be prepared to confront them again in future discussions. The important point is to label their controlling transactions while they are performing them. Here are some ways you can confront controllers:

> You've been talking about your idea for eight minutes and
>   I'm concerned that other points of view aren't being
>   expressed.
> When I'm (or another member) talking you seem to be
>   interrupting.
> You're interrupting.
> You're bringing the discussion back to your idea. Have we
>   discussed this enough, group?

Blamer Interventions

Although blamers will rarely admit to a mistake or failure, they almost relish casting fault on others. If any group members constantly blame or complain, the first intervention is to have them provide more information to support their point. Second, ask other group members for their perceptions. Present your perceptions of the event or person being discussed. Have the group discuss one specific issue at a time. Don't let blamers scatter the focus of the group by changing the subject with a different complaint or individual to blame. Keep the discussion focused.

If blamers continue to blame and complain, even relishing the additional time and attention the group has provided them with first interventions, you need to change your strategy. Call attention to their blaming behavior by directly labeling the transactions: "You're blaming again" or "You're complaining again." See if this changes their behavior. If not, confront the blamers as a group and share your feelings about their behavior.

It is never easy to correct blaming behavior. The best you can do for the group is to bring the behavior out in the open by labeling the blaming transactions. There's something about bringing behaviors into the open that can help to modify blamers' behavior.

Pleaser Interventions

Pleasers agree to just about anything for the sake of peace and tranquility. When people constantly placate and attempt to please other group members (usually controllers), modify their behavior by playing the "heavy." Usually, when pleasers please or placate, no one intervenes and the cycle is reinforced. Challenge pleasers by stating positions and making demands that are the opposite of what they are agreeing to. No matter what the pleasers agree to, take the opposite position (generally against controllers) and see what the rest of the group does with your intervention. Your goal is to throw pleasers off balance by not agreeing too quickly with their characteristic behavior. Continue this intervention when pleasers try to please.

If pleasers continue to please despite your interventions, you can employ a different strategy. You can label their transaction and invite a different perception by saying, "You are being too agreeable. Are there any weaknesses or disadvantages to this proposal?" Many times, just saying that people are "being too agreeable" and asking them to note any weaknesses is enough to cause them to pause and take a second look.

Distractor Interventions

Distractors will attempt to sidetrack the group's work. They will joke, flirt, or question the importance of the task. They are often the court jester, the class clown. For an occasional tension release, distractors are fine. But as a continual disturbance, their behavior can be frustrating and detrimental to the group's functioning.

The best way to deal with constant distractors is to ignore their diverting comments and request that the group return to the discussion topic. Remember to label the transactions by saying, "You're distracting us from the topic at hand. Can we return to our discussion?" Be swift in making your request to return to the discussion after distractors make their statement, even though they may object to your being "too serious" or "too uptight." Ignore humorous or sarcastic remarks from distractors; simply make your request to "return to the discussion."

If distractors refuse to cooperate by continuing their distracting behavior, bring the matter to the group for discussion. Share your perceptions of their distracting behavior and how you feel about its dysfunctional effect on the group. Ask for feedback from the other group members. Most likely, distractors will use humor or divert the attention of the group by shifting blame to something or someone else (namely you for being too serious). Your interventions should be able to modify or eliminate their distracting behavior.

Ghost Interventions

Like a silent face in the crowd, ghosts sit there in the group and say nothing. The cause of this behavior may be stage fright, lack of commitment, apathy, or a host of other explanations. But the result is always the same—nonparticipation or absence. Yet their impact on the group's task effectiveness and social atmosphere can be devastating.

Of all five dysfunctional behaviors, the ghost is the most difficult to prescribe an intervention for because of the various reasons that may be causing the behavior. Without going into a more involved and detailed discussion of these reasons, I'd like to suggest some simple guidelines for dealing with this behavior:

> Encourage the ghost (silent or low-verbal member) to share
> an opinion.
> Compliment the ghost for any contributions.
> Take the ghost out for coffee after a meeting. Be friendly.
> Confront the ghost for not following through on duties.
> Confront the ghost for not attending a meeting.

If ghosts continue to be silent (or low-verbal), maybe that's their personal or cultural style of communication. There are individuals who are, by nature or past experience, more reticent than others, and you have to find gentle ways to encourage their participation. There are also individuals whose cultural or ethnic backgrounds differ in terms of interaction expectations. Many cultures regard direct eye contact, personal remarks and requests, and individual achievement as undesirable and objectionable. Be sensitive to these differences in cultural perspective and try to discover ways to invite and promote participation in the group.

Ghosts can be the most difficult to deal with accurately and effectively. Be tentative, gentle, supportive, and sensitive with them, but enforce rules that govern completion of tasks and attendance. Neglecting responsibilities and absences from meetings cannot be tolerated indefinitely. If in doubt, be kind but firm.

These five dysfunctional roles may arise occasionally in your group. The behavior of those exhibiting any of these roles will normally be mild and subtle, requiring only one or two interventions on your part to modify or eliminate them. But if the behavior is extreme, exaggerated, or physically threatening, appropriate steps should be taken to release the individual from the group.

FORGIVENESS

A subject that lies at the foundation of your work with others in small groups, especially in the area of conflict, is forgiveness. **Forgiveness** is the act of granting free pardon for an offense. In essence, it is the act of letting go of the desire to get even, to make someone pay for the hurt he or she might have caused you during some disagreement or conflict. It is also the act of asking someone to forgive you for an offense you may have caused.

In any group process, people's efforts will often fall short, circumstances will not always accommodate the best-laid plans, and your feelings and those of your group members will eventually be hurt by some incidental or catastrophic event. When hurt by someone, be it by a critical remark or an act of betrayal, we experience the initial feeling of shock, dismay, or a host of other uncomfortable feelings. But eventually, each of these feelings gives rise to anger—the anger of being injured by another individual.

> One forgives
> to the extent that one loves.
> FRANÇOIS DE LA
> ROCHEFOUCAULD

When we are hurt, we will ultimately experience anger. We can do one of two things with this anger. We can hold on to the anger or we can let go of it. We will explore ways to let go.

When we hurt another person, guilt is most often the resulting feeling we must live with. Guilt for a remark made in anger, an expectation we cannot live up to, or an act of deception. No matter what we did to bring pain to another person, guilt is our eventual destination if we don't make amends with the one we hurt.

Whether we are prisoners of our anger or prisoners of our guilt, we are held hostage by these powerful feelings until we decide to let go of them. The only way I know to be free from their suffocating grasp is the act of forgiveness. But to forgive and to ask for forgiveness requires an abandonment of your usual, familiar way of dealing with hurt, anger, and guilt. Use these principles of forgiveness to let go instead of getting even.

Forgiveness is a decision, not a feeling. An erroneous concept regarding forgiveness is that you should feel like forgiving someone before you communicate your forgiveness of the offense. Forgiveness has nothing to do with your feelings. Forgiveness is a decision to consciously let go of your guilt or anger. Initially, forgiveness has more to do with your head than your heart. Don't use the excuse that you don't feel like asking for forgiveness or forgiving someone for an offense. Forgiveness is not a feeling, but a decision.

Forgiveness requires suspension of the ego. As I stated earlier, your decision to forgive or ask for forgiveness is difficult. It requires that you suspend your ego, putting yourself second. This is not an easy process—to occasionally suspend our preoccupation with ourselves. Yet it is essential to the act of forgiveness.

Forgiveness is a never-ending process. Whether we have made the decision to ask for forgiveness or grant forgiveness, the process of forgiving is a never-ending task. Forgiving is not a destination. Rather, it is a way of traveling. It is actually something we become over time—a forgiving person. Forgiving demands of us the greatest of all tasks: the willingness to permit others, and ourselves, to make mistakes.

Asking for Forgiveness

If you have wronged someone in your group and want to ask their forgiveness, try the three-step AAA Forgiveness Technique:

> **A**dmit you were wrong.
> **A**pologize for the offense.
> **A**sk for forgiveness.

Let's assume you criticized another group member unfairly during a meeting. The following day you feel guilty about your critical remarks. You decide to ask the individual for forgiveness. This is how the AAA Forgiveness Technique works:

You:	Nathan, do you remember the meeting last Thursday?
Nathan:	I've been trying to forget.
You:	*Well, I was wrong to criticize you in front of the group.* (admitting you were wrong)
Nathan:	You bet you were. That was a terrible thing to do. Would I ever do something like that to you?
You:	No. Probably not. But *I apologize for criticizing you. I'm sorry.* (apologizing for the offense)
Nathan:	Apology accepted, I guess.
You:	*Would you forgive me for criticizing you?* (asking for forgiveness)
Nathan:	Well, yes. Of course I'll forgive you.

Not all attempts at asking someone for forgiveness will go this smoothly. But did you notice how you admitted you were wrong, apologized for the offense, and asked for forgiveness? This AAA Forgiveness Technique can be very useful in dealing with your guilt over something you have done. It can bring you to a place of forgiveness, and that's one of the nicest things you can do for yourself. Remember— be gentle on yourself.

Forgiving Others

When someone has hurt or offended you, your initial response can range from mild surprise to rage. Eventually, your hurt can turn to anger. What you do with this anger will determine, to a large extent, the kind of person you will become and the quality of all your relationships. If you choose to hold on to the anger, you can become bitter. If you choose to forgive the person who hurt you, your anger will dissipate. You don't want to be holding on to this anger, for it will only hurt you in the long run. Here are some ways to forgive others.

Forgiving those who are not apologetic. There will be occasions when someone hurts you and is not apologetic, let alone repentant enough to ask you for forgiveness. Forgive this person anyway.

You may not want to forgive this person initially. In fact, you may never feel the desire to forgive this person for the wrong. But, remember, forgiveness is not a feeling. It's your decision to be free of the hurt and anger someone else has brought you. You can use three methods to forgive those who have hurt you and refuse to be apologetic.

Pretending to forgive can be used when the hurt is too recent or too serious for you to even consider a decision to forgive the other person. Here's how the technique works. You place two chairs about three feet apart, facing each other. You sit in one chair and imagine the person who hurt you in the empty chair. Next, you pretend you have decided to forgive this person (even though you have not really made this decision) and you tell the other person in the empty chair you have forgiven the offense. Picture the other person's face softening as you say the words. Imagine the other person saying something thoughtful, considerate, or even apologetic. After you have told the person you have forgiven him or her, just sit in your chair and feel your response to the exercise. Do you feel the same? Do you feel a slight change? Do you still feel the hurt or anger?

The **imagining their death** technique involves imagining the person has only one day to live. Even though this individual is healthy, happy, and still not apologetic, you are to imagine that the person has only twenty-four hours to live. In twenty-four hours, the person will be dead. Do you feel the same? Do you feel slightly different? Do you still focus on your hurt? Or are you thinking about the other person? Have your feelings changed about the relative importance of the offense compared to his or her impending death? You'll be surprised how this will change your feelings toward the person.

With **direct forgiving**, after you have decided to forgive the other person for an offense, you share this information in person, face-to-face. The primary weakness of this method is that the other person will often respond with denial, justification, rationalization, or blame. The person may even deny he or she did in fact offend you. No matter what response the person chooses, emphasize the fact that you have chosen to forgive him or her for the offense. You don't have to be the best of friends after the meeting. The single purpose for the meeting is for you to let the person know you have forgiven him or her.

Forgiving those who ask for your forgiveness. If someone who has hurt you comes to you and asks for your forgiveness, you should forgive that person, no matter how you feel. Remember: forgiveness is not a feeling, but a decision. You need to forgive the person to be free. If you decide not to forgive, you, not the other person, will carry the weight of anger and resentment.

Forgive those who ask for forgiveness. It's really the only choice you have if you want to be free. Forgiveness may be the most important lesson you'll learn while you participate in and lead small groups.

Conflict is a natural part of all group discussion and of life itself. Rather than avoid or intensify conflict, you can choose to address it directly and constructively with gentleness and caring. Your willingness and ability to build bridges to those who are disagreeable or hostile, and meet them with openness, fairness, and even forgiveness, can change them. See conflict as an invitation to create common ground, to bring peace, and ultimately, to be more loving. There can be no greater creation in small groups.

INDIVIDUAL AND GROUP EXERCISES

10.1 Boundary Making

Communicate a boundary to an individual whose behavior is unacceptable to you. Select someone from your personal life (spouse or partner, parent, child, best friend, acquaintance) or professional life (coworker, supervisor, employee) who did or said something that bothered you. Arrange a two- or three-minute meeting with this individual and share your boundary. Complete this premeeting form before you meet with this person.

1. Who is this individual?
2. What behavior is unacceptable to you?
3. Construct your boundary statement. If you____, then I'm prepared to ____.

When you share your boundary with this person, provide some brief introductory remarks about the situation before you communicate your boundary. The purpose of the meeting is not to blame or punish, but rather to inform the individual what you find unacceptable and what you are prepared to do if the behavior is repeated.

How did your meeting go? How did you feel composing your boundary statement? How did you feel asking this person for a meeting? How did you feel communicating your boundary to this individual? How did the person respond? Have you noticed a change in the person's behavior since your meeting? How can you incorporate boundary making into your small group?

10.2 **Group Conflict Resolution**

Have your group members use some of the procedures outlined in this chapter the next time they experience either a procedural or substantive conflict. Assign one group member to identify any procedural conflict the group experiences and act as the facilitator to resolve the conflict. Assign another group member to identify any substantive conflict and facilitate the group's interactions during that conflict.

10.3 **Group Role-Playing**

Meet with a team of five classmates. Assign each group member a different dysfunctional role. Have one group member role-play the dysfunctional behavior in a problem-solving activity. After the member has role-played in the activity, the other group members attempt to modify the person's behavior using the interventions suggested. Repeat with another group member and dysfunctional behavior.

How did your group handle the various roles? Can you see yourself actually using these interventions in a real-life situation? Why or why not?

Afterword

You shape the lives
of those around you.

CATHERINE PONDER

The dinner guests were lined up saying good-bye to Gary and Tricia at the front door, thanking them for the marvelous evening. It had been a lively gathering of Gary's engineering team from work and their spouses. Vicky and I were invited to the dinner because I had coached his engineers in small-group communication skills during the previous quarter.

After walking the last guests to their car, Gary and Tricia returned to the house and plopped down on the sofa, insisting that we sit down and visit.

"That was a fun time," remarked Gary. "We would never had gotten together had it not been for those workshops of yours and Lee Nguyen's comment that I needed to be a better listener."

I remembered Lee's comment. During one of the group's heated sessions, Lee told Gary to "listen to your team without interrupting so much." Gary's face reflected the surprise and the sting of Lee's remark, but the group had developed an atmosphere of unusual openness and trust during their time together and Gary received the feedback.

Gary not only heard Lee's words, but he also began to change the way he interacted with team members by letting them finish their sentences—many times listening for minutes without interrupting. That's one of the reasons why I liked Gary so much; he genuinely wanted to improve the way he communicated. Gary's dinner party was just one of many ways he tried to understand and connect with his team members more.

"I remember Lee's comment," I replied.

"That comment changed Gary's relationship with our daughters, too," Tricia said with a smile. "For the past few months Gary hasn't finished one of Shannon or Laurie's sentences or walked away during a disagreement. He's really trying to be a better listener at home."

"I'm not perfect, but I'm getting there," added Gary.

"We're all trying to get there," I whispered to Vicky.

During this lifetime, you will be given countless opportunities to participate in small groups. Whether it's facilitating a problem-solving team at work, organizing a charity fund-raiser, or planning a vacation with your family, you will be involved with helping many groups reach a variety of goals.

In your efforts to participate and lead more effectively, remember that every comment and every behavior can influence and shape the group's interaction and productivity. The more openness and trust group members develop, the more successful they will be, not only in terms of achieving the group's goals, but also in improving their personal lives. You may even inspire a father to be a better listener to those he loves.

You will make a difference in every group in which you are involved. Will your contributions add to the distraction, confusion, and conflict that plague so many groups? Or will your participation help encourage, guide, and even inspire your groups to success? You will make a difference. The important question is this—What kind of a difference will you create?

Bibliography

Chapter 1. Working in a Group

Bales, R. 1976. *Interaction Process Analysis*. Chicago: University of Chicago Press.

Fisher, B. A. 1970. "Decision Emergence: Phases in Group Decision Making." *Speech Monographs* 37:53–66.

Fisher, B. A., and D. Ellis. 1990. *Small Group Communication: Communication and Process*. New York: McGraw-Hill.

Hirokawa, R. Y., and M. S. Poole. 1986. *Communication and Group Decision-Making*. Beverly Hills, Calif.: Sage.

Poole, M. S. 1981. "Decision Development in Small Groups I: A Comparison of Two Models." *Communication Monographs* 48:1–17.

Senge, P. 1990. *The Fifth Discipline: The Art and Practice of the Learning Organization*. New York: Currency and Doubleday.

Shaw, M. 1981. *Group Dynamics: The Psychology of Small Group Behavior*. New York: McGraw-Hill.

Schutz, W. 1994. *The Human Element: Productivity, Self-Esteem, and the Bottom Line*.

Chapter 2. Discovering Yourself

Adler, R., and N. Towne. 2000. *Looking Out, Looking In*. Orlando, Fla.: Holt, Rinehart, and Winston.

Ellis, A. 1998. *A Guide to Rational Living*. Englewood, Calif.: Wilshire.

Moore, T. 1992. *Care of the Soul*. New York: HarperCollins.

Stevens, J. O. 1990. *Awareness: Exploring, Experimenting, Experiencing*. New York: Bantam.

Storr, A. 1993. *Solitude*. New York: Free Press.

Chapter 3. Expressing Yourself Clearly

Hayakawa, S. I. 1964. *Language in Thought and Action*. New York: Harcourt Brace Jovanovich.

Satir, V. 1988. *New Peoplemaking*. New York: Science and Behavior.

Tannen, D. 1986. *That's Not What I Meant!* New York: Morrow.

————. 1991. *You Just Don't Understand*. New York: Ballantine.

179

Chapter 4. Listening for Understanding

Axline, V. M. 1967. *Dibs: In Search of Self.* New York: Ballantine.

Floyd, J. J. 1985. *Listening: A Practical Approach.* Glenview, Ill.: Scott, Foresman.

Gordon, T. 1970. *Parent Effectiveness Training.* New York: Wyden.

Tannen, D. 1986. *That's Not What I Meant!* New York: Morrow.

Chapter 5. Problem Solving in Groups

Bormann, E. G. 1990. *Small Group Communication: Theory and Practice.* New York: Harper and Row.

Dewey, J. 1910. *How We Think.* Boston: D.C. Heath.

Gouran, D. S. 1991. "Rational Approaches to Decision-Making and Problem-Solving Discussion." *Quarterly Journal of Speech* 77:343–358.

Hall, J., and W. Watson. 1970. "The Effects of a Normative Intervention on Group Decision-Making." *Human Relations* 23:299–317.

Hirokawa, R. Y. 1985. "Discussion Procedures and Decision-Making Performance: A Test of a Functional Perspective." *Human Communication Research* 12:203–224.

————. 1988. "A Descriptive Investigation into the Possible Communication-Based Reasons for Effective and Ineffective Group Decision-Making." *Communication Monographs* 50:363–79.

Hirokawa, R. Y., and M. Poole. 1986. *Communication and Group Decision-Making.* Beverly Hills, Calif.: Sage.

Poole, M. S. 1981. "Decision Development in Small Groups I: A Comparison of Two Models." *Communication Monographs* 48:1–17.

Schultz, B. 1996. *Communicating in the Small Group: Theory and Practice.* New York: HarperCollins.

von Oech, R. 1990. *A Whack on the Side of the Head.* New York: Warner.

Wood, J. T., G. M. Phillips, and D. J. Pedersen. 1986. *Group Discussion: A Practical Guide to Participation and Leadership.* New York: Harper and Row.

Chapter 6. Preparing for Discussion

Beebe, S. A. 1995. *Communicating in Small Groups: Principles and Practices.* New York: HarperCollins.

Roszak, T. 1986. *The Cult of Information.* New York: Pantheon.

Wilson, G. L., and M. S. Hanna. 1993. *Groups in Context.* New York: McGraw-Hill.

Chapter 7. Guiding Discussion

Benne, K., and P. Sheats. 1948. "Functional Roles of Group Members." *Journal of Social Issues* 4:41–49.

Johnson, D. W. 1987. *Joining Together: Group Theory and Group Skills.* Englewood Cliffs, N.J.: Prentice Hall.

Chapter 8. Leading a Group

Barge, J. K. 1994. *Leadership: Communication Skills for Organizations and Groups.* New York: St. Martin's Press.

Bass, B. M. 1985. *Leadership and Performance Beyond Expectations.* New York: Free Press.

Fiedler, F. E. 1967. *A Theory of Leadership Effectiveness.* New York: McGraw-Hill.

Greenleaf, R. K. 1990. *The Power of Servant-Leadership.* New York: Berrett-Koeler.

Hersey, P., and K. H. Blanchard. 1988. *Management Organizational Behavior: Utilizing Human Resources.* Englewood Cliffs, N.J.: Prentice Hall.

Schultz, B. G. 1996. *Communicating in the Small Group: Theory and Practice.* New York: HarperCollins.

Schutz, W. 1994. *The Human Element: Productivity, Self-Esteem, and the Bottom Line.*

Stogdill, R. M. 1974. *Handbook of Leadership.* New York: Free Press.

Wood, J. T., G. M. Phillips, and D. J. Pedersen. 1986. *Group Discussion: A Practical Guide to Participation and Leadership.* New York: Harper and Row.

Chapter 9. Building a Cohesive Group

Bormann, E. G., and N. C. Bormann. 1988. *Effective Small Group Communication.* Edina, Minn.: Burgess.

Fisher, B. A., and D. G. Ellis. 1990. *Small Group Decision Making: Communication and the Group Process.* New York: McGraw-Hill.

Janis, I. 1973. *Victims of Groupthink.* Boston: Houghton Mifflin.

_____. 1983. *Groupthink: Psychological Studies of Policy Decisions and Fiascoes.* Boston: Houghton Mifflin.

Shaw, M. 1981. *Group Dynamics: The Psychology of Small Group Behavior.* New York: McGraw-Hill.

Chapter 10. Managing Conflict

Filley, A. C. 1991. *Interpersonal Conflict Resolution.* Glenview, Ill.: Scott, Foresman.

Fisher, R., and W. Ury. 1991. *Getting to Yes: Negotiating Agreement Without Giving In.* New York: Viking.

Jandt, F. E., and P. Gillette. 1985. *Win-Win Negotiating: Turning Conflict into Agreement.* New York: Wiley.

Shaw, M. 1981. *Group Dynamics: The Psychology of Small Group Behavior.* New York: McGraw-Hill.

Index